SALLY PURCI

Sally Purcell

❧

Collected Poems

❧

EDITED BY PETER JAY

PREFACE BY MARINA WARNER

ANVIL PRESS POETRY

Published in 2002
by Anvil Press Poetry Ltd
Neptune House 70 Royal Hill London SE10 8RF
www.anvilpresspoetry.com

This book is published with financial assistance
from The Arts Council of England

Designed and set in Monotype Bell by Anvil
Printed and bound in England
by Cromwell Press, Trowbridge, Wiltshire

ISBN 0 85646 338 8

. . . Y sobre todo tendrás
los regalos de mi pecho,
las finezas de mi amor,
la verdad de mi deseo . . .

Contents

DARK OF DAY (1977)

from BY THE CLEAR FOUNTAIN (1980)

from GUENEVER AND THE LOOKING GLASS (1984)

LAKE & LABYRINTH (1985)

FOSSIL UNICORN (1997)

Preface

'SALLY ANNE JANE Purcell' was the way she was always known to me, at Lady Margaret Hall, Oxford, where we lived in the same building one year; we were also both reading the same subject, Modern Languages, and had Rhoda Sutherland, a passionate French mediaevalist, for our tutor. The dance of Sally's first names (dactylic?) followed by the two stresses of her surname (spondaic?) seemed the perfect way to capture the musicality and mysteriousness of her presence, the quick head and long tendrils of hair, and her drifting but intent walk, which had worn down the high spikes of her shoes so that the toes curled upwards. She also had read so much and inhabited so many writers' and poets' imagery that it felt as if more than one name was needed to do justice to the multiple layers of her imaginative life. I was very drawn to her, but a little alarmed, too: she was fey.

One night, she agreed to cast a spell for me (I was suffering from unrequited love) and told me to come to her room late, because it was necessary that everyone should be asleep before the charm would take. We sat on the floor and lit candles and she found a grimoire she had – it was the first time I'd heard this witchy term. It was all very quiet in college; nobody seemed to be stirring near the chocolate or cigarette machines, the chief haunts of our night life then; it wasn't exam time, so not much need for midnight oil. When we checked the quad, there seemed to be no lights on. And so she began weaving the words, in Old French, on to a paper on the floor, using the book.

It didn't work; after a few days, I had to admit my case was without hope. Sally Anne Jane said we must have missed someone, who had been still awake and so had spoiled the spell.

I learned from this several things, which haven't faded. I had experienced the split consciousness of the receiver who believes and does not believe at the same time, for the magic was enthralling and filled me with hope even though I knew that, even as we solemnly performed the love knot, we were only playing (*only* playing?), laughing at the whole thing, enjoying spending these thrilling quiet hours of darkness together. I don't think Sally was surprised either by the disappointment of the outcome: she was always focused, as it were, on the stone which Dr Dee scryed for secrets, the obsidian disk he used, not on the secrets he may or may not have found there:

> Stone, pure as it left His crucible,
> is hidden still within each grain of dust,
> . . . we snatch or forge
> moments when that world shows through . . .
> ('Dr Dee (IV)', p. 150)

We had snatched one of those moments.

The dedicatee of the first two collections of poems collected here, 'Alasdair', must be Alasdair Clayre, I now realise, and he must have been the friend through whom I heard of and came to know Sally Anne Jane, personally, beyond the college and subject contacts. He too is dead: he killed himself in 1984, throwing himself under the train at Chalk Farm tube station. Sally, Alasdair and another friend, Peter Levi, who died two years after Sally, shared her intense identification with the subjectivity of Greek lyric and of Provençal song, with myths and alchemy and divination. They staked their existence on poetry, and, like sea creatures spinning their shells, inhabited 'the ruined /paradise of language'.

This person of many words and many books who was the poet Sally Anne Jane Purcell contains many chambers, some dark and muffled, others light and airy: rooms of tragedies and epics and lyrics and travellers' tales and fairy stories. Some even hold forests – the dark wood of Dante, the dark pathless forest of Broceliande, the briar thickets of the Sleeping Beauty; others open on to a solitary figure – Persephone in the underworld, or a woman holding a thread, like Ariadne. As she writes in 'Oxford, Early Michaelmas Term', she wanted to 'increase the delight in imagined possession /of the inherited magic world . . .' Learning isn't the right word because it sounds dry; Sally's prodigious range of allusion is light-fingered; and always voiced through her own unique sensibility. Her wide knowledge lives in the delicate mesh of her language, and does not make it droop.

The mediaevalism of the early collections coalesces into a Gnostic vision of existence, which confers on poetry itself the power to bring back the lost dimension of unearthliness, as in the vision in 'From Bernard Silvestris' (p. 135):

> Uncounted crowds of souls
> . . . cling, weep desperately,
> knowing
> they are condemned to fall
> out of splendour into dark . . .

It's in poetry that heavenly things live: her lines are lit up by jewels and wonders, crystal and emeralds, ethereal, bright beings – the Phoenix, for example. Sometimes, the lost zone of imagined light fashions emanations in this shadow world: the fossil unicorn of the title in the 1999 volume. This is an impossible wonder, a never-to-be-seen relic – a fossil unicorn! – and it reconciles fantasy with actuality, sutures the split between the existence of the imagination's objects and their fated Eurydice-like evaporation. Sally Purcell magicks the mythical beast into being as a matter of historical record – a scientific remain, a Victorian naturalist's proof. The poem in which it appears acts itself as a shard, and its fragmentary delicacy prompts the reader to recreate the larger view, the vessel from which it was broken off.

The fossil unicorn appears at the close of a poem called 'Robert Kirk'; the connection between the seventeenth-century divine and the creature's imaginary trace reveals the poetic method of Sally Purcell. For Kirk, the author of *The Secret Commonwealth*, was a Scottish pastor, writing in Scotland after the Revolution, and one of the earliest and most comprehensive witnesses to the reality of fairies. Furthermore, as the poem reveals, he unwillingly became a part of the lore he unfolded, when he was abducted by fairies one night out walking on the moors and failed, despite his pleas from his captivity in elfland, to be returned to the world of mortals.

Kirk is one of the many inspirational ancestors Sally Purcell has gathered in a kind of Parnassus of her own that ranges from Virgil to Pessoa. One of the most finely wrought elegies in that last published collection speaks in the voice of Ovid from the

Black Sea, where he was exiled for trespasses unknown, by the emperor Augustus; another enters the spirit of Michelangelo as he thinks of his beloved Tommaso Cavalieri, the object of some of his love poetry, and here the stimulus to two of Purcell's most packed and limpid lines. They catch at Michelangelo's self-identification with Saint Bartholomew, flayed in martyrdom: 'And in your sudden sunlight / my old skin lies in heaps about your feet.'

The poems seem to me to grow stronger, with some of the finest of all among the uncollected found after her death. Here, flickering changes of mood and strong feelings energise new departures, such as the laconic delight of 'N-Town, *c.* 1500', with its wonderful entries from the accounts of a passion play ('Payd for a pair of gloves for God'), to the intense lullaby 'I love you like a small tidal river . . .' (p. 192):

> Lie gently in your natural harbour,
> my bones the breakwater . . .

She also seems to gain in hope: the Gnosticism that perceived this world in darkness yields at times to a mystical, passionate sense of immanence. This deepening faith in salvation perhaps derives from long reflection on Christianity (she was a quietly practising Catholic most of her adult life):

> Healing light overflows from an empty grave;
> God's body is a crystal; whole or broken,
> every part of the crystal is full of sun.
> ('Easter '87', p. 186)

Themselves translucent and ethereal – like the diaphane in which Robert Kirk saw the fairies embodied – Sally Anne Jane Purcell's lyrics repay meditative reading, giving up their mysterious secrets slowly but richly.

MARINA WARNER
Kentish Town, 2002

Foreword

IN A RARE WAY by contemporary standards, Sally Purcell knew
the path her poetry should take and held firm to it. Her first
book is still fresh and young but no more than a handful of
pieces in it might not have appeared in her last. The cumulative
effect of her collections is of a deepening concentration, the
elaboration from different angles and refinement of a tapestry
in which every thread bears her clear but unobtrusive stamp.

Her poetry, seemingly indifferent to shallow notions of rele-
vance, creates a world whose trappings are very distant from
our own, but at whose centre is a questing vision. Its truthful-
ness lies in the psychological and spiritual accuracy with which
she draws her characters' conflicts and predicaments in their
approaches to the eternal quest. Its beauty lies in her attention
to language and her unique personal music.

She was poet, classicist, mediaevalist and translator. She
died at the age of 53 on 4 January 1998 after three months
mostly unconscious in hospital. She had collapsed at home with
what at first had appeared to be a stroke. In fact she had a
lymphoma of the brain cells, so rare that only some 100 cases
are recorded. She left her body to medical science and died with
£200 to her name.

She was born on 1 December 1944 into a working-class
family, descendants of the composer Henry Purcell's brother, in
Aston Fields, Worcs., where she attended the village primary
school before going to Bromsgrove High School. Inspired by
her teacher David Rudkin, the playwright, she excelled in
Greek and Latin, though she chose to read Mediaeval and
Modern French at Lady Margaret Hall after becoming the
school's first girl to win an Oxford open scholarship. She was
also offered one by Cambridge, and could afford to be amused
that she did not attain the standards required by Durham.

At Lady Margaret Hall she took a second-class degree in
Mediaeval (a spelling she always insisted on) and Modern
French. Somewhere along the way she had also become a first-
rate classicist. She was much involved with the university's
Poetry Society and began publishing her distinctive poems in

undergraduate magazines. It never occurred to her to leave Oxford after graduating. She spent several years on the thesis that brought her an MA in 1970 but decided against continuing with a PhD.

In her hand-me-down Lancing College jacket and with her small hippopotamus tucked permanently under her arm – it was with her in hospital – she seemed the kind of eccentric whom only old university towns can support. In speech, she never used contractions: it was always 'I do not think', never 'I don't', and her delivery was evenly accented, almost as if English were French. In others all this would have seemed an affectation; in Sally, who was diffident although not insecure, it was just her particular style and quite without ostentation.

She was at home among scholars and writers and was as erudite as any of them. She rarely left the environs of Oxford, and almost never travelled abroad. Among her favourite buildings in Oxford were the Taylorian, the Duke Humphreys Library in the Bodleian, the nearby Kings Arms and the Duke of Cambridge in Little Clarendon Street when it was a pub ('Ted's'). And there was also 'Wain Towers' (I am not sure if this was her expression, but I think so) when John and Eirian Wain lived on Wolvercote Green. Pubs were as much markers in her life as they are in Edmund Crispin's Oxford-based detective stories which she loved (she was also a Wodehouse devotee). Sally lived by and for books. Her lack of interest in the quotidian meant that she watched no TV other than horse-racing and cartoons, did not listen to the radio or read newspapers. She did not understand how bank accounts worked and never had one. Latterly she became partly reconciled to telephones and learned enough word-processing for her freelance bibliographic work. But she continued to need occasional reminders that others did not always share her Latin or Greek.

Her spiritual habitat was really somewhere between the thirteenth and sixteenth centuries. Oxford allowed her to scrape a living on its fringes, not always congenially, but she never complained. Careless of her material well-being, she was meticulous and conscientious in all her work. For years she lived partly from typing: theses, which she admitted to correcting whenever their grammar pained her or she spotted a wrong reference, and several of John Wain's books. She was a barmaid for years at the Kings Arms. She did bibliographic work for Simon King's Military Policy Research project and freelance proofreading of scholarly volumes for the Voltaire Foundation, where her deep scholarship was especially well deployed and respected.

With her immersion in the classics and the writers of mediaeval France, Italy and the early renaissance, she was always at odds with our time. Vulnerable as she often seemed, she had the inner resources and underlying toughness to manage such a straitened way of life. Her inner life was, I think, very private. Despite some shyness she was, if not gregarious, at least happy in company. She loved a 'hooley' and had a well-developed sense of mischief to go with her sometimes boyishly vulgar streak. As a student she once caused parental consternation by posing for a nude photograph which graced the pages of *The People*.

But the core of her life was in her mind and her spirit and their learning. Her poems reveal her concerns but give few biographical clues. Usually cast in the form of intense, concentrated dramatic lyrics, their matter was generally drawn from classical, Arthurian and mediaeval myth, but cumulatively they created a striking and haunting imaginative context which is still hard to analyse. 'Ghostly music' and 'diamantine elegance' are phrases from an early review by Clive Wilmer that suggest her qualities. To the reader prepared to cast aside our age's more workaday preconceptions of what poetry should and should not be, her poems – if enigmatic, even hermetic – can be enthralling.

Fossil Unicorn (1997) was her first collection in ten years. She had corrected the final proofs but the book appeared just after she went into hospital, too late for her to be aware of its publication. Conscious, she would have been delighted and then have got on with something else. I remember the late John Wain, who admired Sally's work and talent, once expressing some exasperation with her for not being more ambitious about her poetry. But Sally was not one to force the pace; she would quietly, privately write (or as she put it, 'commit') poems only when they came to her, and then she would not think of publishing them unless someone asked her for new work. Her genuine diffidence was matched by complete respect for the mysteries of the art. I think that John Wain's complaint, with which I sympathised at the time, seems less valid in the light of this collection (a great proportion of which he would not have seen). Sally's diffidence was not lack of true poetic ambition; it was indifference to her worldly literary reputation.

She had lived with her companion of 22 years William Leaf, the last ten years in Cumnor. She was a faithful friend who took pride and joy in the achievements of others and was always supportive of their endeavours. She was a delightful being.

She produced four main collections: *The Holly Queen* (1971) and *Dark of Day* (1977) from Anvil; *Lake and Labyrinth* (1985) from Taxvs, and finally *Fossil Unicorn* (1997), again from Anvil. Her other work included translations: for Carcanet Press a selection of *Provençal Poems* (1969) and Dante's Latin treatise *De Vulgari Eloquentia*, published as *Literature in the Vernacular* (1981); and Hélène Cixous's *The Exile of James Joyce* (1972). She also edited and introduced selections of George Peele and Charles of Orleans, and of D.G. Rossetti's *Early Italian Poets*. With Libby Purves she co-edited an anthology of young poets, *The Happy Unicorns* (1971).

As a translator, Sally was in general (though not exclusively, as several pieces in this book suggest) a literalist. She believed that translations should convey exactly what was said, and the languageless reader simply had to imagine the rest, that it was hubristic to hope to recreate the style and give the substance too. So her translations tend to be rather plain, with her poetic instincts held in check. Except, however, in her version of Nikos Gatsos's long poem *Amorgos* (Anvil, 1998): she responded to this poem's combination of the classical and the folkloric with a beautifully delicate and crisp translation. Characteristically Sally, who did not claim that her modern Greek was on a par with her ancient, said that the version was largely Peter Levi's work, but he said differently.

This book contains the complete texts of Sally Purcell's four main collections, together with the poems from two booklets, *By the Clear Fountain* (Mammon Press, 1980) and *Guenever and the Looking Glass* (Greville Press, 1985), which were not reprinted in subsequent collections.

The uncollected poems are from two groups of typescripts and a small amount of fair-copy manuscript found in Anvil's files, supplemented by several batches of fair-copy manuscript lent to me by her close friend Simon King. I am grateful to him for allowing me access to these papers, and for preserving what he was able to retrieve from the house she had lived in. The material in these collections overlaps considerably with her last two published books, but has provided the whole section of 'Uncollected Poems'.

To my very great pleasure I found among the uncollected material not one poem which I thought should be excluded. More importantly, there is a good number of very fine poems which had barely seen the light of day. There are several versions of some poems, and it is sometimes not clear which she would have preferred to see in print, but these variations are rarely significant. From my own experience in publishing three of her books, I can say that while she was always open to editorial suggestions, she was also very clear about the poetic intention or structure of a given poem.

There are numerous small textual differences between the various printed and manuscript versions of poems. The Notes record any substantial departure from the printed versions. Generally I have preferred the latest version of a poem, where that could be determined. There are few indications of dates on any of these papers; such as exist are given in the Notes. Almost all of the manuscripts post-date 1985 – or even perhaps 1989 – but that does not of course mean that all the poems do.

Many of the poems are untitled, and these are uniformly given here with the first phrase or line followed by ellipses. Otherwise, the titles are her own. I have regularised their capitalisation as it varied from book to book, though some inconsistencies remain. Foreign phrases, which she often gave in lower-case as titles, now have initial capitals. I have left unchanged her distinction between the forms 'and' and '&', the latter representing the unstressed form. Stress marks over vowels in '"In every word shine many lights"' and in the Lope de Vega version are from her manuscript.

As it was her practice to include translations and variations in her books, I have not hesitated to end with a small miscellany of versions from pre-modern poets. Apart from her versions of Greek epigrams, these come from the unpublished papers. There are other translations – two poems by Jean Fanchette from the '60s, for example; and a letter to me mentions further translations from Vittoria Colonna, which have not come to light. Her separately published version of Nikos Gatsos's poem *Amorgos* is very fine, and the interested reader will also want to look out her collection of *Provençal Poems*. But this book primarily celebrates her own work.

The epigraph to this collection comes from a file-card in Sally's handwriting. I have not managed to trace its source; it might be from an anonymous ballad, or from Lope de Vega. It means, roughly, 'And above all you shall have / the gifts of my heart, / the essences of my love, / the truth of my desire.'

PETER JAY
Greenwich, Easter 2002

The Holly Queen

(1971)

FOR ALASDAIR

Queen Proserpina walks . . .

Queen Proserpina walks
    through late autumn;
the glowing fruit of ice
    that she holds
covers the dying sun, & chills
    all ripeness to the bone.

The pomegranate that illumines
    all streets of the dead
sheds gorgon-light on every richness;
    yet the waning day & creatures,
knowing Her untouched by pity,
    still invoke her gentleness:

'Allow us, lady, a small time of warmth
    against the frozen Hand of Glory,
and some few kind illusions
    kept from summer's wreckage,
a brief & sudden breath of flowers
    in this mortal winter.

Bale-fires on the dark moor . . .

Bale-fires on the dark moor
    light your journey between the worlds;
here may one meet the mighty dead
    beside the central pool
& find the making place
    in the wood whence all things grow.

    Let yourself learn
from the great shades' language,
    called through the flying air –
this the heart had always known,
    although, on returning,
it remember never a word.

    The wood stands eternal –
follow others who were lighted
    to the never-changing place
whence you may reach all worlds,
    and recognise your source, the well
of the golden head that sings.

    The wood stands eternal –
follow others who were lighted
    to the never-changing place
whence you may reach all worlds,
    and recognise your source, the well
of the golden head that sings.

The King is Dead

The witches' wheel spins in a net of trees,
reeling skeins of water out
through the bitter air;
Ixion hangs upon the turning wind,
encircled by an icy cord
coiled out long before his birth
for the year's royal victim.

As rivers lose their names into the sea,
his blood marks all the scarlet leaves.

Hyle

Remotissima est yle scilicet materia prima
(GROSSETESTE, *De Causis*)

As from mirrors glimpsed in empty houses
and from the safely blind wall
from the ring of standing stones
a patient silence watches, biding Time;

the sun has no place here,
could speak no word to make
          the stone trees rustle
or move their dark branches;
the sun must fall silent
          in the icy waves of this primeval grove,

the Centre of the Wood whence all things grow.

Verses for Tapestry

to Sally and to Nicolas

Only by a mirror
can the unicorn be snared,
desire seeking the ungraspable
object of worship – faithful reflection of self.
Holding the solemn, pretentious mirror
the lady knows this well –
as the prowling lion or satyr cannot.
Tranquil unicorns are trapped
by calculating virgins;
the mirrors reflect on innocence
and weary purity.

Three Voices

I At the freeing of the springtime waters
embroidered birds and snakes
come down from the tapestry
to move through living leaves

II Vulgarity in pink and yellow
perches where the golden bird should rest
it is not this year the magic appears
– but rich toys cannot compensate
for the ever-broken promise

III Forgetting disillusion
each year prepares again
for the anticipated phoenix.

ii   Perhaps this year the promise is
that destruction will at last be accomplished:
the sun turning black as a wolf's throat
and Thor stretching vast from the clouds
to shatter the icy moon and the seven stars.

iii   The bladed wind is murderous –
as, when the quest is ended, prince or girl
must kill their faithful servant the fox
to snap the spell, restoring his human shape –

i   But this time unreality may win,
tapestry and window change places,
and I reach that island where the unicorn dances.

Terra viventium

Braving the cataract where his world ends,
the cartographer sails towards Paradise Terrestre;
gryphon, dragon, skiopod or magic tree
detain & merit his attention, cannot long divert
the solitary fantastic traveller
                             driving on
to that solar wood where unfallen Adam,
Phoenix, & all pure colours live, beasts talk,
& solitude is a double chime of joy –
his goal the undreamable centre,
Hesperidean oranges beneath chill leaves,
                             the whirling dark:
to seek in antiquated maps
a poem not of this making.

Sarras

So, having come to seek
the city founded on the waters
& set in rivers' winding ring
like an Isle de Voirre whence none return
Galahad, Percivale, Bors, drew to her bright haven
who dances on the light of hidden seas.
The glassy-green & Circean illusions rejected
had brought them to this echoing shell
of the hermit's tranquil clarity,
where the winds are still;
opening before them, the spiritual palace
adumbrated those mysteries they had followed
through darkness,
which a man will not find
unless he bring them, in his heart,
from the quest's beginning.

Lancelot Speaks

I never saw
God's ghost bleeding in the scarlet grail
though many lost life and reason for a glimpse of it:
that Whitsun the wonder appeared to us
we saw for an instant through the mirror
into a veiled aenigma
and once at Carbonek at the angel-served Mass
I saw a great part of my desire
on a table of silver, clothed in red samite,
and lay therefor dead twenty-five days.
But Galahad my sin-borne son
conceived in treachery at the Castle Case
when the moon was dark
and my body's drunken ignorance blindly trusting
    the queen,
– he achieved that limitless light,
he saw perfection and was not.
I who had knelt to Guenever and God
lay trapped in a shameful bed
as lies like iron bars rose round me.
Pelleas' daughter, servant of the holy things,
gave the greatest riches that ever she had,
and the light of my brain was blown out like a candle.
Galahad the virgin, price of my virginity,
looked on the hidden light, in Sarras,
and ascended to the palace of the spirit;
at Carbonek I knelt, and he blessed me.

Loquitur Arthurus

rex quondam rexque futurus:

hair like talons, fingers hooped with silver,
the dark blood of blackbirds burning in her eyes,
the witch Morgause beside the stairs
was a caryatid of darkness,
its only light her rings

        her eyes

like a haunted child I feared that staircase,
where nightly the king's procession passed – mine –
in a stream of gold and candle-flame
while the witch Morgause waited in the shadow
for Mordred's birth, my necessary

        unknown sin

how could I foresee the Herodian sacrifice,
the shipful of children I sent to drown – for him –
the breaking of the Table, and Guenever lost?
Facing him at Camlann, where the light of Logres died,
I saw complete the pattern sprung from myself

        and the queen Morgause.

The Holly Queen

In this time of the fading sun
strange knights have ridden from the misty shires,
from the withered cliffs of the sea
where death's crimson tower stands,
from magic lands where the trees are of emerald ice,
to my court in the holly woods,

whose berries are the blood of that slain king,
broken by a routing boar or shrieking Maenads,
equinoctial sacrifice, head of oracle's wisdom,
for whom the oak weeps mistletoe,
& nature gives royal valediction
in prodigies and signs of the doom.

Magician Meditating

I *Logres*

The mortal City cannot abide,
nor those constructions of human mind
which it observes,
centuries of unworded loves
& coral-building of courtesy;

Mordred or Ganelon strides through the daylight City,
waiting to break the sapphire sun
down to tarnished glass,
destined to betray the King's creation
as surely as death is ripening within him.

II *Nimuë*

Among invisible trees
her glittering hands keep a freedom
never eclipsed by the envious wizard
who would seek to bind her to darkness;
like a roaming cat she dances
by woods and beaches,
finding gold in earth's veins.

Deceptive as the noonday forest
she seems to offer innocent, uncomplicated charms;
he who believes them will, in a mind's flick,
be wandering lost and sun-crazed there,
a prey to half the devils –
and she will make me trust her.

Merlin from the timeless prison sang
like a great bell heard through trees:
In autumn's fever I fade unseen
& the cave's chill breath will scatter
my leafy words abroad.
Dodona's prophetic oak, Sibylla's oracle,
Apolline laurel by the speaking spring,
feel tardy sunlight flicker through the wood
and prepare now for their journey
to the drowned winter world
where gleams the mortal golden bough.
Dead gems will light me down
to dim waters of the west;
yet if I might return, would Merlin choose
the balas ruby or the storm-blown tree
for burden of new songs?

Sidhe

for Paul

Unborn, unmourned
she moves through the dreamer's world
where a druid star calls
beyond your blessings;

from his carven halls she draws him
to the bleak uplands of Vision,
the glimmering mountain and chill runes
that enchant his half-sleep,

madden his waking judgement.
Let him not scorn the goddess
not the seas & rocks of scarlet
where she leads his true dream.

Baldur

Fettered he lay in the wood of corpses,
Baldur, the young god, whose death held no returning,
under wet, coalblack branches that stand in Jurassic sun.
Cave & fountain, hawk & wolf,
all nature had wept, but the Hag alone,
refusing tears, had made his death immortal.

You leave us but the crying sea,
the poisoned spring, a broken garden,
wolves and storm till the world ends.

Lord, our hopes wander a lost road;
vipers wind through ribs of hall and tree
& the new leaves grow up through your hands.

Walk a winter path . . .

walk a winter path between two rivers
where a white sun hangs trembling;
death sleeps on the water
and his dreams brood in the trees –
this is your return
to a place without ripeness
when fear hangs in the branches
and the stream writhes fast beneath you
too late you will know
that the circle is drawn about you
and the sleeper has wakened.

To N'Azalaïs

Not forgotten in the cold time
when life shrinks to a lunar ghost,
ruins & pathways reappearing
now give stranger signs & patterns –
difficult of recognition,
for covering snow has changed all roads.

Already solemn, the new sun orders journeying,
unwinding pale spells to conjure
the dead hand that kept us bound
in the shivering, bell-hung night –
& troubles our uneasy sleep
with the hunting gale & the sea.

Imráma

. . . bitter salt of apples from the sea
and harshness of splintered driftwood
is all they find who begin
this perilous voyage

the muse medusa caresses her body,
glories in her flesh firmness,
smiles at the promises they assume
who believe in her advances

reflectively she smoothes her skin
and says, I am golden;
languidly worshipping herself
observes anticipation shipwrecked

self-appointed poets wonder
what has gone wrong

Variation n

for Sheelagh

Hecate's mad May branches
tarnish the sane sun,
eclipse the golden buds;
the sky overbalances
into a river full of quietness
and spring beds lovers in the leafy rain.

Tarot XII

for Virginia

The dead man walking on the wind
the Hanged Man in the sun
and my dead midnight child speak all one voice
There are no words to that dark wailing
that cries along all waking years
it will not make me mourn the springtime child
in this cruel season
The Hanged Man bleeding on the sky
swings above a rising sun
leaves are blown down Dead Man's Walk
my withered shadow runs before the wind

Cheiromant

From a yellowing palm she tells
all lands and kingdoms of the heart,
unravelling disaster or predicting
new fantasies of promise
– and times of wandering captive
in the house of Daedalus.
The parchment crumbles as she reads
these trivia in the eye of time;
our one fate stands eternal
and plain as the bone beneath.

Baroque Episode

With measured concentration
Mingling blood for love's token
He hopes to symbolise affections' depth,
Achieve the untenable equation
That added selves make one,
And seal in a small bottle changefulness.

The alchemist's wound is deep;
Black candles gutter in his dreaming mind
And the sleeper is mocked by his adoration's object
That remains with hands unmarked
Outside his gilded iron circle
Refusing to abdicate from its own self-worship.

For Endymion

I

Clouds of dust rising on little-known roads
as the patched autumn departs;
Lovers brush off dead leaves
      and wander home
      still solitary;
Frozen saints hitch their robes tighter,
closing stony eyes to ignore
winter's hasty and unhallowed bedding.

II

O love, when he hungers in the withered autumn,
be for him my fruits of summer,
      that he may
rise through layers of dream at morning
to summer orchards, crimson grapes,
      of my creation.

Note on May Morning

Hoping perhaps to see the very Venus herself
they keep her vigil in the black fields
by the polished river;
her copper star burns in the dawning water,
and holy Latin salutes her day,
tries to exorcise her power of anarchy.

King Cormac's Wisdom

This clarity of air surrounding
trims all outlines of the season
to its own topiary, perfect;
feverish lucidity soon to die
refines to alchemical concentration
grass and copper and yew,
the three lasting things.

Speech from an Unwritten Parable

You that would burn on the wind flaring over the world,
beggars who cry at the doors of twilight
to ears that the dust has blocked,
cry for the stony bread, love's ransom,
to misers caged in cruelty,
wander in the petrified chalcedony forest
finding no fruit under marble leaves
nor water in the granite –
pity us the starving possessors;
it is your charity we need, your body's poverty.

John Evangelist

Hope came late and I feared
my tongue would wither in the waiting,
dry in silence before I tasted the book
that was bitter within me;
houses dwindled, men died, and I waited
for truth in the thunder flash
in the island of myself
I knew the noonday devil
and the fantasy of midnight
but terror's dimensions fell about me
when I the Mother's foster-son
saw placed on opposing sides of love
black tree and fatal fruit
– body writhing like a serpent on it –
apples on a green tree.

Stripped of amulets' protection . . .

Stripped of amulets' protection,
wander the midnight city
where painted walls declare an older glory
& setting suns a vanished race of kings;
consider the sly grave gaping
as your dead with silver shields descend
– but already the barbarians hack at your gates,
& how should pride remember
Icarus who said
'The sea of air will beat about my wings'?

Margery Jourdain

Those who hold the rune of Hel
outstrip the lightning's flying sun,
stride over gulfs of air;
we brave that solar wheel that spins
at the gate of uneasy tombs,
know the waters where stars can drown.

Others have passed through the bracken-flame
to sounding darkness –
filled with voices, the sky
thickens on their fat smoke –
and tomorrow I must follow;

but above the moon's cold moors
my shadow flies.

Mistranslation

(Etienne Dolet, 1509–46)

Tradesmen and soldiers, poor audience for a scholar,
and corner boys with eyes agape
watch the carrot and radish flames fingering the stones.

A king's protection was relied on once too often;
so ashes twist in a stormy wind
and they sell no food today in the Place Maubert.

Totentanz

Friday, it stormed all night, thrashing about
like a troubled man in crooked sleep,
or crashing drunken through the corridors,
slamming doors, kicking windows.

Then retired to lurk round a wall,
growling like Grendel,
to deal the turning traveller a blow
that shaped him like butter
and shook out on the whirling wind
his fluttering scarecrow rags,
                      the bone
stripped in the pale glare
of the cracked moon.

But at fevered chilly morning the wind dropped,
the bones drooped to rest

                  with a small
rustling sigh of contentment.

Sebastian

In the white garden of your flesh I walk,
where stiff black stems' winged flowers vibrate;
you are so far away and do not know.

You shall have my starry breasts and peach-flesh
and I take on your body of red ruin;
but let me know your peace.

Small Cold Poem

All that night fell
splinters of ice,
wounding the gardens,
and our warm bodies clung together, greedy,
not heeding the cold.
But when we woke
I found my heart
stuck full of them and freezing
like a painted Baroque martyr.

Fragment of Alkaios

(from a 2nd century papyrus)

Hebros, loveliest of rivers,
going out past Ainos to the purple sea,
pouring down from Thrace a shining flood of surf —

many virgins stand beside you,
bathing with tender hands
                              their smooth-skinned thighs,
pouring your waters like a soft ointment . . .

Time Stops

The soft light crying
like fires in a noonday field
and the lovers
lying close in cynical disillusion
feign sleep to prolong the deception
that they are happy and deceived
— spying who shall first pretend to wake.

Invocation

Cushion-hipped Ceres who
hold the chain from desire to birth
(o lady of brightly painted pagans)
and Artemis, daughter of green purity,
extinguish among us the prepared sneer, the underdog's
    pose;
provide an idol in this world
for those who weep by the wall of glass,
and quieten the resentful dead.

Oxford, Early Michaelmas Term

Impossible to register
each delicacy & shade,
each further richness of affectation
this feminine season adopts
for an audience captivated in advance
& hypnotised by hearsay, by skilful propaganda,
by its longing to play Hamlet
and be *really* melancholy.

Confident flirtations with a preciosity
already near to over-ripeness
increase the delight in imagined possession
of the inherited magic world;
whose soul and typewriter will vibrate first
to appraise in College garden
some sere and yellow leaf,
as the aesthetes flower gently?

For S.

Harlequin leaves that cut
A dancing pattern on the maze
Outline daedal floor and forest-woven labyrinth;
Newly ordered, precision gleams,
No longer shadowed by the changing moon.

They must belie the bright work's image
Who build the year's dark scaffold as they fall.

Dark of Day
(1977)

FOR ALASDAIR

Frontispiece

Juventus falls asleep in May time
under a flowering tree in the garden of fables
& the book he was reading,
allegory woven of Grail or Rose,
falls from his hand as the dream begins.

'Through drifting cloud appears that other garden –
I know the carvings that posture & warn
on its walls, the old man seated at the gate
who interprets dreams and symbols I shall meet,
and at the maze's heart one central tree,
the Rose of this world's love
– or the Dry Tree of Redemption, bearing
Phoenix that knows no death.

'And I, Lancelot, old Adam,
hear hermits gloss
images of that sacrifice,
may long for the shrivelled tree
where God's blood flamed,
shall never unlearn the Rose.'

Ariadne

Within the glowing maze Ariadne stands;
a buried city forms her dance's pattern,
her labyrinth is founded on the ruined banks of Troy.

Out of the bittersweet air she leads him,
the king who dances through his fate
in Troy-game, the unchanging order.

His long-told story ripens to an end,
he passes through the final glaring splendour,
and the ancient threads are wound again,
                              rewoven.

On a Cenotaph

> . . . *le cadavre adori de Sapho, qui partit*
> *Pour savoir si la mer est indulgente et bonne*

The sea will weave its light into your long dream
where Orpheus' head gives oracle & prophecy,
borne here on a bitter wave,
& still in summer dawn you will hear
the roaring waters cry.
Hoping to unriddle
the folds of sea or mirror, their brilliant sterility,
withdrawn from the common sun you voyaged
out from the white headland,
following a dark winter's moon.

We stand in cold and ruins, for our spring will never come.

After any Wreck

Here
we have come at last
to a place out of the wind —
we look down from the doorway
of a small stone hut,
peer through mist and drizzle
for the lost sunlit land

and know
that there the waves are gnawing polished beams,
night is fallen on bright columns,
and the sea-sifted weed
floats tranquil over golden tiles.

In this hard refuge
on a hill above Atlantis,
hear only how
a cry from the despairing sea
is broken on the wind.

Tristan

After the sea came the wilderness,
the forest of Broceliande –
one moment out of time on a charmed sea,
becalmed and shining between worlds, was enough
to enslave me thought and will,
to bring me to this coil & tangle.
Your ocean gives horizon, flat clarity, meaning,
and whorls each alone in his hollowness like a shell,
but leads into those thickets of the Wood
where form & horizon perish, where Iseult
becomes an outlaw's mate
and the queenly seat is empty.

I cannot sing to sunlit air,
but I carve my rune on the hazel bough
in this wood of Morrois that holds me.

Early Irish Picture

Along the edge of night
moves the saint who has chosen his path
      of rejection,
to be traveller & stranger wandering
beyond the glass-green rim of the sky
      to seek his kingdom.

Brandan has sailed for his golden Isle,
Columbanus taken this world for pilgrimage.

II

From the sun's holy tree, oracular oak,
moves the servant of the moon,
      rejecting other images,
pursuing his white martyrdom,
the lunar design that is clear
      in its darkness.

He comes alone to a secret land,
between cold marsh & ruined garden.

Two Kinds of Magic

A clouded moon mask
looks into the wood
where a dead king flames brightly;
the sun has lapped his blood,
the crackling forest
feeds on him in darkness
– and lights flare pale among the Roman city's bones
where enchanters draw the future from tombs,
with spells force an empty mouth to speak.
The puppet corpse returning moves
reluctant to the necromancers' word;
he cannot let them know that living magic, how
the red king burning like a fox
has poured his blood into leaves and earth.

Yggdrasil

Withdrawn to his inner citadel
the Emperor can savour at leisure
this irregular season,
watching the swirling mist & leaves,
gyrations not prescribed by ritual.
Panegyric is replaced
by the stormy wood,
its voices through the boughs
calling on the death of richness.
No torches or musicians
divert his thought from this waning;

the night journey and bitter cold
trouble emperors with common fears.
And in the dark he can hear
one dry tree groan,
shuddering,
the Tree that props the world.

All Hallows

The black branch glistens,
weeping yellow leaves
along the watery night;

blood flows back into the ground,
trees' torches flare and die
in the last festival of fire.

The hollow wind strips all green,
leaving only ivy and the mortal yew;

in the stone a toad is alive,
silently preserving his jewel.

Some voice will survive this cold,
to celebrate the autumnless garden.

Merlin

Merlin sang the solstice' rod & rage,
dreaming of a prelapsarian garden
where branching sun confers
a stately clarity
on unfallen word that dances.

His incomplete mortality gives him clearer sight
into the rose or amethyst garden –
but we are of the destroying storm
that whirls us unrepentant through cloud
away from the ruined
paradise of language;

we glimpse its dream or ghost again
whenever man like Merlin sings.

Nature Note, March 1971

Flowers where no leaf yet stands
promise that eternal springtime
of heart and garden
that turning time
proves again a lie;

the pale bush
will not bear stars for fruit
this year, only berries,
and they will feed mere blackbirds,
not the phoenix from his heaven-tree.

Ars Longa

Alchemical fire burns through a shifting dapple of colours
to achieve its perfect ruby,
bringing forth golden work, a tree bearing suns.
In the mystical marriage of King and Queen,
ripening philosopher's gold in the heart,
we follow the soul on allegorical roads
to seek & map the elixir or the poem,
we need the athanor, the devoted life, crystallising
power of Solomon's ring and throne.

II

Within the fire's bright crystal
where Salamander blazes rosy white
lies our labyrinth's heart, the perfect Stone, in
cataract and spinning storm of gold.

Plain earth, or lead, or fallen man
the alchemist reforms into their single design,
bringing forth seeds of the sun
hidden deep in each dark body;

he disengages from every metal
that within it striving to become gold,
unearths & shows in clear strength
links of a buried unity; here poets learn

how to hold the burning-glass of words.

III

Flamel sought through a treasury of images,
following power in purity, learning over decades
to pluck the mature gold
from its royal tree;
slowly the great colours wheel
out from death's night
through their peacock zodiac
to reach after patient years of fire
a glory that can turn the sea to Sun.

Abelard Solus

Natus est de virgine
sol de stella

Maria, bitter virgin,
diamond sea-star
hung in the chill wastes of air
above this gleaming level
where no sword will ever flash,
my harsh maidenhead cannot praise
your perfect state
for I have known the solar fire
& burned in its heart
till I scorched my life and hers.
Although my red is turned to white now
in this desert of water and air,
despoiled by rebel & savage,
I stand in your silver light,
can have no worship for the freezing stars.
In a world now dead my songs for her
were sung through the morning town;
now in the pure Paraclete her nuns rehearse
my sterile theorems of God.
The sword has fallen truly
between us,
has divided me from what I was,
and there is no returning.

I cannot again be priest of that sun.

For Andrew

Streams that glitter through new grass
flow from a fountain winter sealed;
now rivers are loosed from the quiet cold
and feed on its bitter snow.

Perceiving a new thaw, poets warily
test bank & dyke, prepare to take the flood
& weave the clear net of channels
that will lead it through the fields.

Without them, waters pour down formless to the sea,
to the blank brightness of a sky,
a dazzle of infinitely moving waves,
to the shore that, opening, leads everywhere,
to exile that is everywhere the same.

The Third Way

We set out early, riding through the day
on the broad summer roads of Logres,
yet further out from Camelot
the paths grew narrower, & woodland nearer.
Approaching the borders of the other land,
one of us – or sometimes more – would start,
glimpsing some dream-creature among dim trees,
very close now; no more familiar wolf & boar,
but faun or centaur would appear for a moment,
then flick away into the undergrowth, leaving us
uneasily wondering whether to doubt
or to speak. It was difficult here to see birds,
and they seemed changed, and knowing.
We came with falling night
to the place where three ways meet,
the Road against Reason,
the Road without Mercy,
the Road without a Name.

And the third way brought us here,
to the Waste City;
demons that obeyed the enchanter Virgilius,
giants, or worse, must have built the nodding walls,
the vaulted palace and huge towers
whose ruin is our silent home;
we cannot read its inscriptions
or decipher its mosaics;
the images of Emperor & City are distorted
as by a witch's mirror or pack of cards;
we find no living soul here
but ourselves, who cannot leave.

Within the great night of magic . . .

Within the great night of magic
wizards move gracefully, sure-footed; can tell
from its pattern
where the diamond glass will crack,
what words infallibly attract
the queenly devil to dance or bed,
what planetary fire streams down
informing talisman or crystal at its hour.

The false magician's bartered self
must run the labyrinth's gauntlet, whirling
deeper to its core, unable
to pause, to will a moment's rest.
At every turn there hurtles up to meet him
a painted, fairground Queen of Cards;
shifting shapes that mock his desperation
hunt him ever down   to the silence where
his own scorched image stands before
a weary mirror webbed with scars.

To the Queen at Nonsuch

addressed to Elizabeth I in the late 1590s

'– The city in your dream (not the one
your imperial builders are already sketching)
is an ivory carving, or a jewel
from your regalia, of pearl
and crystal and amethyst, or an illumination
against a flat gold sky from a Book of Hours,

but outside your wall are rings of land
under the grey sea-mist
where witches christen cats and raise the storm
to kill a king,
where servant-girls dance for the Devil
and a farmer's wife shifts her shape to cat or hare
till she come home again; there

is no precision of detail, no delight in elaboration
of beauty –
ugliness of word and action
matches the intent.

The witch that cripples and blasts may appear
as only a mocking obverse to your dream;
but your brocaded ritual may become
self-absorbed as her jagged turning,
may hypnotise and strangle –
beware your obedient creation, and take care
that it be true.'

At South Leigh

In the supernatural wind
that whirls his white cloak, ruffling
great gold wings –
the fierce angel of sword and balance.

Beyond him gape the jaws
of darkness' old dragon,
and above like sparks in smoke
teeter crooked flying horrors.

Untouched by the gales that thrill his feathers
Our Lady stands above her silver moon,
star-crowned and wearing the small sun,
prays for the shivering soul.

The doctrines of courtesy interweave
all creatures in replacement, intercession;
the picture speaks of a lost certainty
to those now who have to unriddle it.

For a Wilderness

Out on the rim of the dark
roam outlaw, Fian, hermit,
who reject your ceremonies
of peacock & pomegranate city,
order and the vine.

Hervör walked among the mounds,
where graves opened all around her
blazing and roaring –
only there in a space between worlds
might she find the dead man's treasure.

Along the lonely edge of waters
Orpheus idly scribbles with a stick
on the sand;
far off a pale sea glitters
& day's waves close over his head.

In solitude the work is ripened,
achieves the blessing.

Lyric

When shall my spring come
and the singing voice   again
praise your rich beauty,
calm delights;

will you hear kindly
such unskilful song,   favour
poor lovers dazed by
your pleasures,

driven to dreaming?
You walk as the sun   that draws
the small clouds after
its shining;

they follow the fire,
bewildered by that   strong love,
know they throng to their
destruction.

Dr Dee Alone

To recall the dead, he says,
is not difficult,
force the tongueless mouth to tell
where treasures lie;
the crumbling figure stammers out its knowledge
beyond our circle's boundary.

By talisman, words of power I teach him,
are bound elemental & daemon
invisible to me;
I dare to unclasp the book
& trace the pentacle, but gaze in vain
into his darkened glass.

Through my learning he might command
that Lucifer, lord of ruined kingdoms;
he might achieve our Elixir,
to re-create (or is it to preserve?)
in Medea's cauldron of memory
the old and dying body.
The immortal mind in that prison cries,

God's mercy let me *see* what I believe and know!

Mosaics

Here our strange madness
begins to find out
the shape dozing in the rock,
patterns of the green holly;
within this point of making, root of dreams,
lie coiled all our possible creatures,
content to be nothing
until the light calls,
since able to be any thing,
able to fly or fall.

Before the roaring trees marched over it
smashing the mosaics' geometry, here stood
a discipline of marble and gold,
printed out its pattern of severe beauty
to fend off anarchy and the biding wood.

Store away carefully the tesserae, coloured and blank,
for one ignored may be the key
of that final design, still unknown;
patiently wait for the crystallising word
to strike jewels from the stone.

Time and the Hour

We returned, expecting the faithful place
to have waited unchanged
in the rays of its long afternoon;
we half-remembered, half-invented, details
of brambles, or a crooked branch,
or yellow apples in long grass; we said,
'That hedge will still be the same'
(forgetting we could now see over it);
'no-one here could fell a tree
or efface a line our memories know.'

Perhaps it was the wrong time of year,
or we had grown estranged;
a cloud-heavy sky rushed upon us, covering
all colour and the unfamiliar shapes.

King Priam is dead with his city
and his lasting monument.

Saturn drags his cold club-footed way . . .

Saturn drags his cold club-footed way
over memory, pattern he breaks, fouls
& scores with leaden furrow;
relics of belief must crumble
at his damp & ragged breath,
tower and altar splinter
before the invading fig-tree's root.

Lamentation for great Pan
faded long ago above a calm,
star-teeming sea,
and the women's voices mourning Adonis
drift into indifferent quiet;
in one place alone they remain,
this luminous abiding city of the mind.

Of Mutability

Here branching bone and the constant rock
are wrought by the waves
into shapes they bear   within eternity's mirror,
regain their inward self, after long wandering.

The island in time's river-ring
is worn thin as the shoulder-blade of a hare
for wizards' divination,
thin as the finger-nail moon.

A bonfire's ashes
glint with shards of glass
grey & silver in the white sun;
great Babylon is a mound of copper dust.

All forms flow down to that one sea
whose rich depth enfolds them,
travel their interlacing roads
to the primal wood, the mid-land-ocean,

where all names rest   in their beginning,
out of the light of sun and moon,
where even Time will come at last
when his day is ended.

One of the Lost Grail Knights Speaks

As rutting summer wearies, and the night
begins to climb stealthily nearer,
the regal sun is travelling down
to scarlet sacrifice;
here sleepy, monstrous-coloured fruits
foam from the branches, or rot in purple shadow –
this is the devilish garden.
Idle, intolerable over-ripeness
lies all around me
these yawning, sultry days,
but even here the bright pain
returns, and I must remember . . .

Once, long ago, I believed
in the Quest; desired that lofty palace
in a land between heaven and earth
transmuting what was mortal.

But I could not breathe its air, I said, nor make
myself worthy; rejecting its grace, I turned away
to choose this poisoned, lying summer.
I dared not take the silent road
past Chronos' tower to the Fortunate Isles.

Sauros

for Paul

Huge beast heaves down through grey saltings to grey sea
as day crawls over a leafless land;
there are no birds yet.
A round horizon's edge cuts down
as water receives him, daylight's hunter.

When his kind has vanished far
into earth's forgetting ages,
he will be Leviathan, king of howling Ocean
who can snap the world in his tightening coils,
power of secret waters & hollows under the earth,

unfathomable, darkness,
who chills our deepest dream.

Astrologer

When autumn's fever half-awakens ancient memories,
when dreams uncoil from their cave in broad daylight
to mingle with its creatures & to cloud the sun,
he climbs again the intricate narrow stair
to his tower room, and follows
Time's journeying, the curving road of stars,

makes ready to cross great Oceanus river
whose waves encircle our tiny world,
to sail beyond the pillars of the sun.

He leaves each familiar boundary,
moves easily through night's hollow vastness
towards ever-retreating Thule,
the pure Hesperides,
or Siren islands white-ringed with bones.

Leaving Troy

Sown with salt, black furrows mark
a dead place where no seed can grow,
grave of our immortal, god-guarded city.

Dragons couch in pride's palace now,
their scales grate & clang on gold
sceptre & jewel tarnishing into earth.

For a few years more we can keep alive
an empty name that stands for nothing here,
until our final exile comes.

My voice blows down the miles of night,
lost among the chill slate colonnades.

Titania

She twirls a blue rose, idly
cracks each bud with her nail
to find its cut heart shrivelled
black by frost; around her
a serene & scented air denies
all snow & ashes of the winter heart,
brittle branch or stream, the falling tower –
these lie outside her proud magic,
warped into painted shadow
by its radiance.

Must my twilight remain that crystal's foil,
is it only fool's gold, Lady, that I bring?

In a twilight between two stars . . .

In a twilight between two stars
your quiet beauty wanders,
among dark streams and broad-winged trees
that stir their feathers in a gentle air;

you listen to shadow's voice here
& the sigh of hidden birds,
when a cold mad moon dances
over green gloom.

Through racing stillness of the sky
her influence thrills down,
marks you out her own
with print of silver seal,

ripens treasure in veins that are
the galleries of her mines.

By this Light

The moon is blazoned in her plenitude
and makes the air with brightness tremble;
empty-handed, all beauty stands in her shadow.

High wisdom in a mist of radiance
is obverse of aphasiac folly
cackling miserly over hoarded husks.

'Wherever in the two worlds you may be
you will find no place empty of my light;
follow my shining myth of lunacy.'

Out from havens of the sun, Domina,
king, fool & poet sail each autumn
for the hidden island of your promise.

Cormac Looks at the Crucifix

Crom Cruach was an idol
axes hacked from bog-oak
black as a toad,
a golden mask on his face
& twelve gods squatting round him.
We gave them blood sacrifice
before the white power came,
with bell and crook and shaven head,
prophesied by druids;
at Patrick's command foul creatures
came swarming out of our gods,
mice and blow-flies, lumps of carrion
scurried, and vanished.

Crom Cruach bowed his hams and died,
falling before the rootless living tree.

Where grass-green starlight falls . . .

Where grass-green starlight falls
upon a winter country,
you can see them, in the distance,
moving, three or four, along the bank
of pallid marsh or corrupted lake,
shapes that drift in a fretful wind,
mere folds in air that trouble sight,
no sound or gesture permitted them
save that swaying in mummified air.

I must travel the land of their despair
a long familiar time.

Wait, learning patience . . .

Wait, learning patience; learn clarity, observing;
admit no forgery; await harsh night
when, most incredible, the word strikes true,
unsought, except through all the labyrinth,
to shock the heart into a strong delight
— to love, a private joy where lies no rest.

Woodchester

Step into this charmed reach
          if you dare;
here Orpheus turns a globe
          of translucent air
strangely solid like ice

where all beasts fall gentle,
          stand at gaze;
fox with peacock, partridge,
          gryphon, thread his maze,
feel no hate or hunger.

Orpheus butchered, headless,
          evermore
sings to sea and mountain,
          within the wind's core
inhabiting stillness.

Electra

'In my dream I stood in a grey land
that had never known tree or sun,
and a little crooked wind blew from nowhere
fretting my hair;
under tarnished heavy clouds
distance or direction were impossible,
no choice could hold meaning.

It was like the salt marshes that creation's gale
streams across in the blackness before day,
but here there was no sea,
here there could be no dawn.

And I slowly remembered fragments
of a life unimaginably distant,
of a child's past, in clefts of time's canyon
freakishly revealed –
my green dress, my toys and games,
all my broken morning.

This is everyman's unknown home, they murmured,
end of journey for stylite and conquistador –
alone before a tomb in a faceless land.'

And all this eternal while Orestes avenger
is hastening down great roads to return to that tomb.

This autumn weather . . .

This autumn weather smokily
          mocks our eyes —
the great leaden bubble of a dome
          flattens into silhouette,
Jack Shadow changes tree to man,
          or casual face to lost familiar,
for a long moment
          of welcome treachery,

wakens into clarity another eye
          that scries truer images
beyond the prisoning cave.

Dark of Day

Jack-in-the-Green solemnly revolves, jigging,
clothed in his nest, a diagram of boughs,
Hooden Horse claps his wooden jaws
as the fiddle unreels rhythmed monotony.

Beyond his figure the third eye sees
divine green kings move destined
along inflexible ritual, spilling their blood
to earth's renewal.

In my End is my Beginning,
for ever.

from
By the Clear Fountain

(1980)

Inside the Pyramid

Inside the pyramid
corridor, gallery, dead-end packed with rubble,
bore through blackness, hollowing out
a night that fears no day;
no moon of air and water
rides by an open window
or calls to plant & beast.
Gardens of Osiris or Adonis
grow green a moment in this dead house
whose ruler shrivels to immortality
with neither heart nor brain.

Our blood is a red coral . . .

Our blood is a red coral
building unknown islands;
no skill of Cyclopean stone
formed this living palace;
Christ is a free man in his father's house,
we are his house.

St Alexis

Clang,
Clang on the boards overhead
Beat the servants' heavy hooves.

Rinds & gristle are my food,
Shoved grudgingly at me
By suspicious hands.

My parents will never recognise
The beggar under the stair –
After so many years
They hope, or see, too dimly –
But there still may be danger
In the wife they chose me (I left her a maiden,
I escaped before dawn, yet she says, 'Take this
for the sake of someone who is lost –
you look like him.')

Lord, may she not hinder
My perfect mortification.

Surfaces

Within the blind wall moves an eye
that looks forever past & through
into its memory of far older worlds
of reptile blood & frozen stone;

cliffs of dark air stand
glinting like mica;
in their hollows writhes the uneasy wind
that crinkles time into wave & whirlpool,
brings the ripe stars down.

Oh walk love's landscape warily,
warily trust its tender narrow sunlight.

Ausonius, *Mosella*, 55 ff.

This river has no secrets, we can look
through the smooth surface to its glassy depths.
As the soft air opens clearly before us
when the winds are still and cannot hinder
eyes that see through space, here we look down
far into the inmost of hidden places,
see things deep-drowned as the stream slips by
and the movement of clear waters
shakes blue-green light over shapes below.
The sand is ridged and wrinkled by the current,
grasses bow and sway on the green floor;
the water weeds that grow there are shaken
by the driving waters, to hide and reveal again
the shiny pebbles, and gravel shows up the green moss.
Like this the shore of Caledonia seems
to the Britons, when the tide lays bare
green seaweed, red corals, and pale pearls, the seed of shells,
for man's delight, and natural necklaces
under the rich waves imitate our own.

Herodias, Dian, Meridiana . . .

Herodias, Dian, Meridiana,
day's devil naked in the forest,
burns like a pearl on the sea-floor
where a tall sun shines.

Beside her that more splendid fountain
promises true knowledge of your thirst.

Ted's

In a drizzle of tingling light
copper-coloured meteorites
made a crown for darkness.
And the wind rode by with his hounds
eternally hunting souls
over smooth black desert where no leaf shines.

Try to sleep, read, invent
distractions; admit
you fear to find
his hoofmarks in the morning.

For A.C.C.

Your sunlight strikes through clear windows,
printing over black & white marble
a net of calm shadow to tame
fantasies of the air.

It moves into heavy jewel-glass,
through crusted rubies
                          to darkness,
down forest-rides of cathedral stone
to die before a ring of candle-flames.

It pours wave upon wave of gold
into the tideless heart
of cold crystal
and grows, leaf and flower.

Pluto's Courtship

Forget your dark anxiety, your groundless fears.
Proserpina; you are going to rule great kingdoms
and to take a husband worthy of you.

I am that son of Saturn whom the world obeys,
whose power fills immeasurable space.
Your daylight is not lost, for we have other stars
and other circling planets; you shall see
a brighter light, and wonder at an Elysian sun.
For us the Golden Age is not yet ended,
our people are blessed, and we keep for ever
what men on earth above deserve but once.
You shall still have grassy meadows, where eternal
    flowers
breathe softer air, flowers unknown in your country.
And in the dark woods is a tree of richness
whose gleaming branches are bent by fresh growing gold,
and this will be your holy tree; you shall rule rich Autumn
and be forever queen of the yellow fruit.
More than this – whatever the clear air surrounds,
whatever earth nourishes, or sea-waves sweep about,
whatever rivers roll along, or marshes hold,
all living things shall bow to you,
all things below the moon, the seventh planet
that wanders the air, and divides mortality
from the undying stars. Crimson kings shall kneel
at your feet, their splendour laid aside,
and mingle in the crowd with beggars, for Death levels all.

[*from Claudian*, De Raptu, *II.277 ff.*]

Propertius 2.27

You are mortal, yet try to discover
death's unknown hour and the way it will come;
you look for horoscopes in a clear sky,
what star brings profit or harm;
shall we march to the Eastern wars, you ask,
or sail to the West – in dark dangers of land, or sea?
Destruction falls on your humble head
when the God of War stirs up confusion;
stay at home – and the house may fall down, or catch fire,
or black poison lurk in your drink.

Only the lover knows when he will die
and how; fears neither storm nor weapons;
he may be sitting in dead-man's boat,
sails hoisted, ready to cast off,
her voice will call him back again
along the road all laws forbid.

from
Guenever and the Looking Glass

(1984)

Guenever and the Looking-Glass

Repeated windows and walls of light
pour down to an invisible sun,
centre of all colonnades of nightmare;
full moon can raise no ghost now,
no flood follow this ebb-tide,
the brightness lies on a gleaned field.
I would not ever understand
why the Quest must claim you –
all it ever did was kill, dazzle,
maim or madden – you did not need
to follow that. I thought you
an opal from Lucifer's crown.

Ailill's Song from *The Courtship of Etain*

Far longer than a year my love has lasted,
lies nearer to me than my skin,
lords it stronger than all destruction.

It can split the world into quarters,
can reach the height of heaven,
do battle with a ghost,
and break his neck.

It is a drowning in icy water,
a race up the sloping sky,
a weapon lost in the ocean,
hopeless passion for an echo,

is my love and my longing for her.

Mermaid

Watery light from deeps of submarine time
streamed round her fluttering in air
when the fisherman lifted her
out of his net;
slowly on land her silver faded,
her strangeness made safe now,
baptised and married,
learning human words.

The ripe moon hangs
like a lamp
in blind man's country
as clothed in matronly black the mermaid wanders
even by tideless pond & puddle
in our world's wood,
seeking the impassible way
back to her lost & simple immortality.

Driftwood, sea fruit, bone . . .

Driftwood, sea fruit, bone
bare, beyond corruption,
scattered among black flint antlers
spell out their hoarded mystery
to heron-legged wanderer or fugitive child,
eyes filled blank with solitude in sunset's chill.

They will burn bitterly green in your fire
that rips & twists yet cannot crack
shape's language, calm purity, whose riddle
you may neither solve nor destroy.

Night gathers round the deeply dreaming stone.

St Antony and the Longaevus

In a dry desolation of thorn & sand
one scorched brown saint
unpicks the city of men, willing
the shape of death
to fret through his flesh and escape.

Out of the enormous light
blackness hoods his eyes;
no human words can move this molten air.
A shaggy beast with cloven hooves
enters the roaring silence.

'Shall creatures of my race be damned?
And can you pray for us?' it calls.
But the mortal cannot tell him,
and the faun weeps.

Gloss to the *Book of Invasions*

From this high tower
look over a sea of bright wind;
hard and fragile walls of glass or air
guard the invisible centre
– here none may land.
The dead patrol these ramparts,
answer no mariner's call
– not easy, to speak to their sentry –
and within, the Wounded King, inaccessible,
unmoving, moves the wheel of the Kingdom.

Nightmare's dark lantern . . .

Nightmare's dark lantern
flickers, revealing
from dead forest or ragged cavern
a glint of eyes like stones,
in wait for the traveller who strays.

Such fear is needful
as inexorable
– poets have always known it to be
tanist and twin of true
vision, its brightness beyond reason.

Views of Loss

Phaëton endlessly falling through air's black mirror
from heights where heaven's arch never sleeps
appears in the lidless Olympian eye
– glaring savage and attentive as a bird –
to drift slackly down into darkening mist
as a drowned man turns & dangles
through tranquil sea-light, treasure-paved.

Earth stares up to receive him, a flaring meteor,
a black-faced comet,
simplified out of humanity by God's fire.

Losing everything, he inherits forever
amber tears from alder & white poplar
and all the ocean's desert for a grave.

A crown of iron & reddening bone . . .

A crown of iron & reddening bone
lies among bramble & weed
where pebbles glint in the sun's treasury.
Vanished every massive stone

that held the royal gold in darkness there,
gates crumbled, noble metals melted,
wind-stripped thorns in loneliness
now guard a King's house of air.

Beheaded, torn to rags, or pierced in battle,
in exile or in Avalon
to heal his wounds,
he has become this high green citadel,
where branch and mound flame out his presence:
in this world he changed his life.

From Cumae

Should the wandering holy isle appear,
& dead sun-gods move about our skies
who are now but sunburnt dust in Pyramid City,
an invisible moon will reverse time's buried tides,
our ever-falling tower
   hang motionless on the wind
and Hades fear for his unconquered rule,
the King of Castle Mortal.

Leuke

In a mirror golden Helen's ghost
remembered . . .
        tawny sunlight of her noon,
        glittering eternity of days at sea,
        flames that clattered through midnight streets,
        one last flurry of sparks that fell
        quenched in ash thigh-deep
        where palace towers had clawed the sky . . .

Always in life she moved
        within a fierce blaze,
burning-glass for poetry & fear;
        she flickers now through twilight air
where frost-white islands turn
        on time's flood;
beyond spinning blackness dream's coast
        lies ringed with splintered bones.

March 1603

The tapestry shivers like a candle-flame
in that little wind cold as a serpent
that creeps from the grave;
the table is a dark river
reflecting silver gleams
that draw night nearer.

An old woman, dying, keeps a sword by her bed
that none dare say, The Queen is afraid,
stabs repeatedly at woven god & hunter
– or the turbulent ghosts behind them –
while their fragile figures move
through her constant looking-glass.

One night she saw her body
'lean and fearful in a light of fire';
her spirit already walks corridors
where her dead are whispering;
only they can say 'must' to princes,
and she will not ward them off much longer.

Loquitur spiritus

Thirty-nine primary colours, in our world,
are shaken from the sun.

What you read as nightmare, in webs of mist,
shadows of a roaring wind,
or scribble on a yellowhammer's egg,
is to us clear message & password.

White roots threading around cracked bone
draw your last design –
immortal, golden, our unfallen tree.

Pythia

Outside, in the sun, bees & blue flowers
grow in flaking sarcophagi.
Humanity's house full of mirrors & bells
has no song for one, Apollo's oracle
who speaks with dead men & daimons
in their cavern of mist, for she,
drawing her nature from both kingdoms,
has chosen the black solstice underground.

Early devils rise & fly . . .

Early devils rise & fly
into an open sleeping face,
burst against cliffs of darkness.

Their bat-cry soars over time,
its needle splintering
incessantly; they lay

slime on the eyes,
foul the river of light.
Daybreak will scatter them in storm,

if daybreak ever comes.

Ark Afloat

Afraid of forgetting how to move
        on steady ground,
conserving our trivial ways
        perhaps for no reason,
we wear ourselves out imagining
        what we may never see,
what will replace the sunken land.

Will there still be sunlight, crops & trees,
        the heavy fleece of summer,
fresh food, and room to walk again?
        When we hatch out
from this wooden shell, will new fears & monsters
        make us long for its prison again?
We shall have to come down from the mountain.

Lake & Labyrinth

(1985)

Lancelot at Almesbury

Here, what was a Queen of Logres
took her to perfection, having lost
everything but one man's worship;
and for two long days, they tell me, her only prayer
was 'Let him not see my living face again'.

I kept my promise, and never saw my earthly joy again
till now – a young corpse, clothed as a nun.
In a place too cold for tears, I leave her
neither cross nor ring
but a branch of white hawthorn.

Time-Shift

A spray of light splashes dark heaven,
of meteor-threads or wild white birds,
plucks one strand of the fiery-pointed web

that holding all things makes them free
within pattern centred on paradise,
a fountain where the cool doves drink.

Merlin (v)

for A.C.C.

Do not stand
between moon & mirror;
to their confident fullness
you do not exist.
Within her eyes, that mirror
constantly the turning moon,
long snowfields uphold a heavy sky,
the river is a snake of black and gold.
A wind full of stars forever hunts
my wraith across that homeless plain.

He stands in his coat of shadow . . .

He stands in his coat of shadow,
waiting, behind a door
before you dare to open it,
at the stairhead or along
your garden path in twlight.

He does not need patience: he knows
you draw towards him
at a quiet pace, inevitable
as the voyage
of mineral in the mine.

Lament for Yonec

I saw him in his own land die
& stain with his human blood
the silver twilit city
whose lord he is; I know
that he can cross the one-strand river,
need neither fear nor count
the bridges passing by;
yet we have shared
this world's time
and here he has never left me.

Dedication

No sorcery uncoils here,
no envious plotting of fallen stars,

but a landscape intricate, harmonious,
lit by its own sun –
by every thought & sight of you
that have made my heart their highway.

'In every word shine many lights'

Broken emerald, diamond splintered,
grate and cut each other to rough sand
till all their light is gone.

Cut into facets, their virtues comprehended,
they wére eyes, divining
tombs of the sun god, mansions of the moon.

Alkestis

She dips, cautiously, into her new element,
practising darkness, rehearsing her journey.
'I shall be counted with those who are nothing,
and never more see clouds dance round the sun,'

she says calmly, and wears away
as a snow-tree melts
to bare twigs and full-rushing water
that suddenly belong to next season.

Dr Dee (II)

Ice that cannot melt,
ichor of the moon,
one stone holds a sheaf of gathered light
no touch may darken.

Deeper than colour, here
my city is founded;
I had sight given me
in the crystal, and I saw.

Born between wood and water . . .

Born between wood and water,
Tristram ran wild there
with no guide but grief;
& Lancelot, when love
had blackened his brain,
lost knowledge of his nature,
became a beast among trees.

Fires without warmth stand scattered
on a dark desert
marking monuments
of hermits having
fled from all faces
to work without distraction
nearer toward the nameless.

Cursed by a saint, Suibhne roamed
far beyond footpaths
out of our warm world,
no food but cool cress
nor sleep, seven years –
he flies through the warring winds,
forever unforgiven.

Solitude builds her city
though the rock resist,
enemies encroach,
poisoned rivers rise;
never more needed
than when shivering storm-clouds
threaten man's mad single eye.

Unending light of golden mirrors . . .

Unending light of golden mirrors
hollows out great rooms within the dark,
vaults & courtyards of petrified air.

While body sleeps the soul may wander here,
but never reach a field or stream
of the lost living country –

this Eurydice must return every dawn.

'I see them walking in an Air of glory'

Hedged around by golden light
the blessed move in labyrinth or procession of prayer
within unbroken Eden,
among living waters & small tame hills
– motionless in mosaic's book of air.
Delight that has roots in the body's
debatable ground
is not here destroyed, but transmuted,
raised to a higher power.

From *Caelica* LXXXVII, The Eternal Glasse

(Fulke Greville)

Everlasting lack of time
lies just beyond the frontier.
One great mirror fills earth & sky,
closing the road, the journey, and time.

Beyond it lies no future,
it has absorbed all distance
to inexorable surface,
gleaming blankness replacing future.

In that mirror move your thoughts,
alive and independent
devilish accusers, shapes of
infinite vexation that were thoughts.

Ripae ulterioris

Edward Thomas learned 'how the wind would sound
After these things should be.'

Merlin foreknew the song he would sing
When the wall of air closed round him.

The heart rises to recognise
That secret lightning, leap into a dark

Whose further bank is revealed to love,
Suddenly, beyond guessing, given.

Aditum per me, qui limina servo,
ad quoscumque voles . . . deos

At frontiers of place or time
where Both and Neither are true
rays of power converge most brightly,
cracks to other worlds open.

The Janus Joseph rules every entrance,
and the hinges of death's door,
borrows a cradle, lends a tomb, preparing
thresholds for God.

Undying priest in the spiritual palace,
he celebrates Mass to bring time
and metaphor to an end –
guardian of Theotokos, guardian of the Grail.

Lucernarium

Before we reach the line where night begins,
where walls are coal-black fog
and light an uncut stone,
Lord, make us moons reflecting
the snow-fields of your illumination.

'The Land of Vision lies full far'

Again Isaac rides to the mountain,
to the hidden height & cloudy stone,
seeking what would have happened,
what secret he would have known
if the crescent moon had ripped him
out of life –
             he moves in its wild waning
to meet his black-faced obverse,
the winter solstice king.

Along dividing lines . . .

Along dividing lines, fence & ford & gateway,
Boundaries of time, November Eve or midnight,
Run green paths to the other world.
Power unearthly as a meteorite
Deepens on magic frontiers –
A ghost keeps every stile.

'Not hard, to slip through the door of air,
That opens both ways; or travel
Into the hollow hill; not hard
To resurrect King Mordrains' land
With a word never spoken, arriving
At no foreseeable time, by no known road.'

Ars Longa (v)

Planets of a subterranean sun,
the noble metals journey into perfection
on paths where every end contains renewal
– pure gold, soft and heavy as lead.

The stones I build with are alive,
and the seeming wanderer
dances a hidden order, transmuting
Adam's earth to radiant ruby,
phoenix into fire.

Lake and labyrinth . . .

Lake and labyrinth inside the stone
lead your mind their maeanders,
initiate's journey to one central cave,
pure as the sea-depths are secret,
unknown to the shouting sky.

Enter,
        be gathered into the stone,
to a spherical horizon,
when the crystal opens and the tides are still
– quickly, before the gates re-appear.

Solitudinem faciunt

Light and water web the oracular sea-cave,
where dead Orpheus' words
drift like Sibyl's leaves.
Fleeing from their song, the hermit moves
alone into dry darkness,
scours away all living slime
to reach the seeds of stone,
pure obsidian mirror
of light for the understanding,
colder than the stars
of black Sagittarius.

Magi moving among the stars . . .

Magi moving among the stars
intricately carve smooth air,
polish and plane it like stone,
under another sun reveal
map and fossil in its veins.

Their tranquil roads of solitude,
almost immortal, run close to ours,
parallel a moment, then swirling out,
comet-like, into the night of years.

Within their crowned glass alembic
reposes a flaw, stain or garden –
the moment of human magic before
Pentecostal cracking and crying of thunder.

Joanna

(Luke 24.10)

Darkness divides unevenly
like floodwater over fields;
frightened women follow
a dry stream's path
among grey rocks,
before the world begins.

Time approaching holds earthquake,
lightning, a sudden angel;
Time will stop, and Adam's chains
break like links of ice.

Proprii aenigmata vultus

We seek the midnight moorland
where Image lives in his tomb;

we fight until doomsday, blackening
a ford of clear water;

we hunt through the triple world
the riddle of this face

involved, involved
in the hidden meaning.

Vikarr

From the tree-top he sees Odin's acre
lit by another sun, over there;
raised like a look-out tower
above the world's wood,
or the high Cross in the land of the Trinity,
our need incarnate endures the moment
when magic mimicry suddenly hardens
& impossible weapons kill –
each new king inherits, for one dark wing-beat,
his vision of winter
under glittering leaves.

Manannan Speaks:

Adam's fall veiled for your eyes
the Land of Paradise ever-young,
alongside and beneath mortality.

Returning travellers may not land
on your death-giving earth
where time accumulates;

in a moment inheriting
three hundred years, they fall to ash
before their tiny weak descendants'

frightened eyes. One more fortunate
yelled out his story from a boat offshore
and fled to break the horizon again.

Ebbing tides of shadow . . .

Ebbing tides of shadow
leave on black sand
rounded green gems
with salt-grey patina;
jet, bright as coal,
revealing phantoms in the air;
amber from Thule,
Merlin's farthest island, all
magic spheres of loneliness.
Their shape is achieved now:
for them there is no more sea.

Dr Dee (III)

He affirms the rich image
into whose lines
the molten starry influence has flowed;
engraves it within him, becoming
a signet, a jewel unflawed,
offered to its ruling Daimon.
His mind moves lightly among living branches,
through all created pattern
ascends
into the central Name, to rest
in the solitary darkness of God.

Every detail of the city's doom . . .

Every detail of the city's doom
was written in statue and column,
secretly, before its foundation;
this was known,
but none could read the meaning.

By crosses, where roads meet,
at well, or tomb, or ford,
the adventures of Logres await
accomplishment;
Galahad is approaching through all time.

He will make the splintered sword
complete, resolve all contradictions,
bring history and enchantment
to an end;
restore unbroken unity, macrocosm

like a bead of sap, or drop of dew.

'And taking leaves all things
in their right place'

(E. Muir)

God, within the primeval waters
a vast face floating in the dark,
holds in solution all memory
and perfect forms of mystery
unawakened
to grace of creation.

Forgive and *reconcile* will need no meaning
in a compassion that knows
every true shape
and abiding judgement,
when God achieves
the enchantments of this place.

Terra secreta

A pale, clear river sliding by grey willows;
a bitter little wind wrinkling the day;
cold black shadows, hard as rock,
stiff reeds, old broken beech-trees –
Virgil prepares his palette:
yew-tree, ivy, pine, all nocturnal green.
The melancholy powers are always near,
even in pastoral's permanent afternoon.

Centuries afar, another Virgil
knows there is another world
underground, where unearthly time
is lit by the light
of a sun and moon unknown.

Luna in lampade

Three Marys on the living sea,
their boat a crescent rimmed with pearls,
clumsily, hopefully sketched
in a scrap of base metal
stained and twisted by age –

as the material of the Stone
is common, unregarded,
trodden underfoot everywhere,
these rough signs, like a seed
falling into night, secretly grow.

The fourth of the three,
the black moon their servant,
invisibly completes the triad, belongs and does not belong,
encircling time's triple kingdom holds
all things in their brightness,
the rich abyss before creation.

From Bernard Silvestris

Uncounted crowds of souls
hurtle before the gale,
helpless like frozen birds.

On the edge of aether's realm
they cling, weep desperately,
knowing
they are condemned to fall
out of splendour into dark,
from heaven's pure eternity
to the thick, mortal air.

Their natural powers paralysed,
memory and innocence gone,
in this blind cell
before they can return to light
they have a long forgetfulness to drink.

Bright mist in mountains . . .

Bright mist in mountains
lies high round the valley,
impenetrably guarding
Phoenix from the world of death.

Around one precious tree
the still air forms
a perfect emerald
(eternity in a creature,
as much as it can hold),
within which moves the constant
breathing of leaf & wave,
each distinct as a snowflake.

No dreams or skeletons
disfigure with changefulness
this golden ground; outside its orb,
where tangled growth begins,

torn clouds & cries
beat endlessly round
a sneering brazen head
that will speak when time is gone.

Eternal image, able to roam . . .

Eternal image, able to roam
throughout the inconceivable,
descended into deprivation
to make earth once articulate
in man's body Christ glorified,
matter given shaping speech
according to His word.

In this place of separation
where buried Osiris blackens,
man's own images may recall
some dignity of their distant source
of harmony in God's mind,
as matter given shaping speech
echoing His word.

After the partial, covered vision . . .

After the partial, covered vision
the grail vanished from the dark shuttered hall:
it would not be contained in our narrowness.
'When this holy thing goes about,'
said a noise behind the King's brain,
'the end of earthly chivalry is come,
the wedding-ring of Logres is cracked;
we shall never meet more in this world,
though I have loved you as well as my life.
You will all go, some to be lost,
devoured by sea or forest,
some choosing that sterile tree
where Death has made his nest,
others going trustfully to sleep in God's hollowed hand;
a few returning, lame or empty-eyed.
The light we have known could not last; we dwindle,
islands in the night sky, scattered fires.'

Twice I have crossed Acheron . . .

Twice I have crossed Acheron,
leaving the sour black wave
untasted; yet everything is changed here –
and perhaps for the first time, true.
I see men as dead trees bleaching,
the flint a drifting wraith,
the sea a shadow
and light a dungeon-wall.
                    I used to be
a sleepwalker in the forest of Day.

Down the long rides flowed sunset . . .

Down the long rides flowed sunset,
blood-red fiords piercing into the wood,
drowning the hesitant fool
              who stayed out too late
on paths that make their own twilight;
no map or portulan could guide,
              no horizon draw him.

Perhaps in that light, near as a rainbow,
to innocent eyes the trans-mortal country
might appear, the place of ambiguity;
one easy miracle from a living man
is all it needs
              to unbind its trance,
heal its royalty, release the waters –
but he stands there still, without a word.

From Euripides, *Troades* 1060 ff.

Zeus has deserted his temple, our holy mountain,
first landfall of the rising sun;
altar and lantern freeze
where twelve golden statues
glimmer alone through the night,
and God our lamp
confers his gift of shadow.

Castellan of a strong headland . . .

Castellan of a strong headland, forever
Build, renew defences out of silt & rock
Against the shifting meadows of olive or turquoise light;
Here only detail and haste are known –
Further out, the historian or another sees
In Time the laborious perfect.

St Columcille

Sunlight piercing his dry hands that bless,
under an earlier creed's holy tree
stands the gnarled scarecrow,
servant of God, proud in his secret
abdications;
he has starved his body, cracked his own heart,
studied torment with passionate care,
achieving power
that can craze this air with lightning, day with dreams.

From Propertius

Let others write about you, or else you can stay unknown;
let a man praise you if he likes to sow the sand.
For believe me, all your gifts go with you,
carried out in one coffin one dark day,
and the passer-by will scorn your bones –
he will not say 'This ash was once a learned girl.'

[*Elegies* 2.11]

Fossil Unicorn

(1997)

THIS BOOK BELONGS TO SIMON

January 10, 1984

Like a river of smooth stones the broad road flows
down to dusk unending, stagnant shadow-pool,
and the locked gate where one ice-cold lantern burns.

Branches clash in a dry wind; the twisting path has left
    him
far from landmarks where we could meet,
wandering in the wood of Celyddon.

Easter '84

Your palace in this world
lay between earth and open sky,
adorned with sun, rain, wind; you saw
into death's glass beehive, knew by heart
the invisible city guarded by skulls
that glint along ramparts & under gateways.

You realised God's pattern
linking all the gardens;
you gave your will entirely
to the terrible journey
out beyond all sea-marks –
to a new grave of clean stone,
home-coming.

Receding into mist . . .

Receding into mist, the burnt fields
carry their scars towards oblivion
& begin to grow new flesh, in secret;
the cold white honey
that embalmed Alexander
piles up in every cell.
Autumn is an island
in the subterranean sea,
its air patterned by bells
          that melted long ago,
its coral or granite ready to perfect
this time an enduring image.

On Propertius IV.7

'Ghosts are something; death is not the end of all;
a sallow image escapes when the pyre is out.
I saw her bend over my pillow when
she had just been buried by the growling road,
& sleep had gone to the funeral
as I roamed the icy kingdoms of my bed.
Her hair and eyes were still the same,
her dress all scorched down one side;
the fire had gnawed the ring she always wore,
and Lethe's acid had just bitten into her lips.'

That ghost of a ring haunts me more
than all the vampire bitterness
that will not let her die.

'And you shall find all true but the wild Iland'

Ariadne regains herself & her solitude –
all she betrayed to the stranger
is vanishing as the black sails dwindle
and he goes forward to found his town.

Where salt-star & rose of sulphur
glitter on the rocks at noon
she has her realm again,
making tiny mazes, Troy-games,
with white pebbles in the sand.

The scapegoat Old Year . . .

The scapegoat Old Year hobbles out
from the westward-facing door
that has opened at last;
time & grief swirl in like the tide
melting a sandcastle.

Drive out the Winter King,
lord of sour pomegranates,
with a weight of dark knowledge
bound to his shoulders –
nail his shadow to a tree.

He is the grain flung out to die, the fool
keeping safe in his wizened heart
what the green hazels know.

He turns from the narrow isle . . .

He turns from the narrow isle of liberty
where he still wears a crown
and flings into the night
where our world thins to a razor's edge
and there may be no more sea.

Beyond lies the bare path
of rejection of images,
through the broken water, into completer darkness,

             'and a song I tell to no man
unless he sail with me'.

Landsmen for an old crime . . .

Landsmen for an old crime
condemned to the sea and wind,
we are borne by our shapeless path
into the final storm's eye
through autumn's rain of blood,
or, one moon-freezing night, cast up behind the castle
where God keeps the door like a servant,
with its iron keys in his opened hands,
where nothing more is necessary
and the road
             disappears

Out from time's tumulus . . .

Out from time's tumulus,
      the black bonds laid on Cronos,
Our Lady comes walking
      with a dish full of light,
light that flows through her fingers,
      wavers, ebbs & returns,
between wandering walls of shadow;
      Maria, gateway to the great sea,
draws near
      like a sound growing clearer,
bringing together at last
      the holly-berry sun
& pearls of mistletoe.

Fifteenth-Century Woodcut

At the sign of Time and the Wild Man
the World lolls & drinks their house wine
beneath an ever-burning bush.

Just outside crenellated cardboard walls
hangs on a hill Scarecrow Skeleton,
whose rags flap & shrivel in the blue-black wind.

Grey flames roll & drum . . .

Grey flames roll & drum around this island,
Jack Frost leaps & shakes his quills,
cuckoo-spit glitters – wizards' weather
hangs a net before your eyes.

You must wade through dew and cobwebs,
through a dance of green mounds
(shifting always, looking almost alike),
and seek in vain unmisted sight,
until time dies in your arms.

Dr Dee (IV)

Stone, pure as it left His crucible,
is hidden still within each grain of dust,
where we can never come;
break the skin of a dewdrop or mercury bead,
the secret flees to a remoter place.

Since the keys of Eden rusted into a blood-red clod,
we snatch or forge
moments when that world shows through,
the innocence it has never lost
– before 'it is gone, with a brightnesse'.

Linquenda tellus

Castle, bridge & fountain,
familiar human print on stone & water,
brief houses of the heart

suddenly turn into a grim Little-Ease;
the forgotten voice of ocean
has drifted this far inland.

And without a word, the inland man
turns, to receive his journey –

a lane with shining walls will curve at last
down into that sea of light,
real home & only rest.

Moor, mound & crag . . .

Moor, mound & crag
rinsed clean of meaning
by starlight,
now you have lost your familiar look
I can leave you,
bury my gems of glass,
start walking into the cold hours,
sure to meet before death's dawn
a cross of wind with arms of darkness,
waters that leave a taste of ice.

Tomis, December

When the numbness wore off and I realised
I was here for life,
I started to thump on the doors of my tomb,
rattling, shouting *Let me in, damn you!*
But they would not open. I stare
down at my bruised knuckles:
Far from home – easily said,
mooed in a maudlin ballad,
but here it cuts like the north wind:
'adrift in a sea with no harbours,
to die on a shore with no name.'

Can there be any future in this blank place,
on the rim of the recognisable world?
Its water, food, soil, air corrode me quietly;
no healing grows here except in my memory.
He spared my life with a view to this dying.

If my shade, or any thing that is me,
escapes the bonfire's crunching jaws,
it will have to wander among hostile ghosts
over this last promontory of earth –
delicate cruelty, that.
Let me return, one day, a small pot of ash & bone,
let me not be exiled everlastingly
from the great lost City;
leaving her was my first and hardest death.

In dreams I fly over my ruined house,
roof & door gaping in moonlight;
I wake and grief stands before my eyes
like a colossal granite god.

Do I need to suffer more?
Somebody thinks I do. My wounds are raw
and somebody wants to pull them open again.
But only a fool insults a grave
or tramples on a rag of shadow.
Hector was a royal enemy
living; the thing Achilles dragged in the dirt
was not Hector; and I am not
the shape crouched in a freezing hut
under a sky like filthy snow
gradually forgetting the sound of its own language,
gradually forgetting trees, grass, birds, the light
of the sun

Poem for Lent or Advent

Signs and shadows
have been gathering reality
as they rush upward
to the surface of time;
they break
into our minds' air, snatch us through
knowledge of the visible,
through the game of images,
into that Love
Who sawed both cross and cradle
out of the same tree.

Merlin's time will return . . .

Merlin's time will return
    on the swirling tide of grace
as heavenly wind & water reveal
    all stone to be ephemeral.
Easter is a fiery golden tree
outlasting the fresh rains of April,
green candles with a blue flame.

A small wind is fidgeting . . .

A small wind is fidgeting round the stair-well
the red moon has turned her horns downwards
your candle has quietly made a winding-sheet
madam said to come and fetch you.

At the door of Castle Mirror
spirals on lintel & threshold
reel in a spider-thread of sound,
prepare an invisible net;

skulls glow softly along the wall,
lapped by lime-green fenland,
forever barren, the last wrong turning.

After Crinagoras

Caves in the nymphs' holy headland,
spring water flashing down rocks,
little wooden shrine
        to Pan of the Pine-tree,
gratefully I add a stone to your cairn,
green island in the shadow of God's thought,
        and travel on.

I'll sing you seven seas . . .

I'll sing you seven seas,
Green skull upon the shore.
What are their memories,
Green skull upon the shore?
Quick sand & dead sand,
False dawn & cold horizon
Ever opening, never closing,
All the wrong cards in one hand,
Which evermore shall be so.

Elizabeth of Bohemia

The sky shines like water above a lake of snow
where a formal garden repeats itself, jarring
into parody, leading to a shapeless fire;

hell-mouth waits peaceful, not content, not impatient,
in the lee of cavernous winter arches.

Rational skeleton in the green tomb . . .

Rational skeleton in the green tomb of spring,
will your meditation on one abiding word
ever quieten the heart?

                        – Never till it can rest
in its natural home, no longer wondering
if the summer flowers will be early this year.

Be not afeared . . .

Be not afeared
      nor confident
when the dragon seems dead,
a handful of brown scales on the ground.

If he has gone to his own place
it is to soak up strength
from crusted pools of bitterness
below the world;

every moment may just have been
his nadir.

The rain . . .

The rain
is a stranger's
footstep in the porch –
some Hyperborean or Inca
that walks on feathers or fine linen,
some dreamer
who has left his body

The wind
is his hand on the latch,
bringing a gift
or a ghost's knowledge

The darkness will be his face

Out from the moon's hillside . . .

Out from the moon's hillside
they drift across our noon-day,
chill the April sun,
rap on windows of dream.
They are forgetting how they ever
lived under this air.

And I can scarcely recognise
grief, now levelled by the tide
invading upland gardens,
the fierce immortal sea.

My heart that wanders in your forest . . .

My heart that wanders in your forest
under the shadows of changing day
sleeps where love like starlight spreads
a colour unknown;
brightness falls like the dust of snow,
to your spring has come the once-wild heart.

Breathing the golden darkness . . .

Breathing the golden darkness
that is their element,
plumed & leafy creatures glow
deep in a forest of tapestry.
A sudden sting of glittering rain
would wake them into our unquiet air
with a shock like love,
irretrievably.

Lie gently in . . .

Lie gently in
your natural harbour,
my bones the
breakwater,
your heart
the moon's
reflection;
tears divide
light into colours –
emeralds
          through the fine rain.

Autocrat of the subtle underground world . . .

Autocrat of the subtle underground world,
he sits waiting for Orpheus the beggar
to scramble down ankle-breaking scree,
past luridly lit waxworks,

and savours the breathing man's pain,
twists & turns like a piece of jewellery
that almost possible condition . . .

But can the god know what gift he is giving,
that silence for a theme?

Sestina for Two Voices

– We slip round the corner of your mind's eye,
Creatures of lonely twilight between hills,
We are never unmistakably seen;
If living men have strayed on to our path,
Our visitation is like that of love
And follows them into their deepest dream.

Where light & shadow variegate the dream,
Leaves of magic trees have dazzled your eye
With every brightness that waits upon love,
Inward-glowing light of enchanted hills,
By which you recognise the coiling path
Which you have always known but never seen.

Then how to understand what you have seen,
Never sure you have glimpsed outside a dream,
Where what you cannot see is the true path?
Is it full clarity within your eye,
Is it the view from frightening hills,
The joy of sight at last made clear by love?

– When this light is the beginning of love
It is like nothing I have ever seen;
It is no view from any frightening hills,
It is nothing I have known in a dream,
But it overmasters my dazzled eye,
Commands by knowledge of an unknown path.

I feel that there is darkness on this path,
And I can guess the darknesses of love;
There will be need for me to trust an eye
Familiar with things I have not seen;
There will be times I hesitate to dream
And times when I am frightened of the hills.

I shall not be rejected by the hills
Although I many times will miss their path;
My journey will take me into that dream
Because my guide will always be my love;
I give myself to what I have not seen
Because all knowledge comes not from the eye.

Gold light streams down hills in Apollo's path;
labyrinths of dream lead at last to love;
and fullness is seen by one perfect eye.

After Amairgen

I am the quiet fruit in your hand
I am the green weed that sways in the current
I am the dark red wrack
that clings to ocean's floor below all tides
I am shell or fossil that can strip no further
I am driftwood after its voyaging
I am the sunlight flickering on these pages
Who but I knows the exchange of sea & shore?

As the wind of springtime touches her . . .

As the wind of springtime touches her
she is transformed, Chloris turns to Flora;
flames of roses run over the earth
which till then had been all one colour.
Time returns; there are no tears now
except to weep for sweetness of love.

Spider . . .

Spider
        walks up sloping or vertical air
Swallow
        slashes a woven invisibility
Fish glides through soft heavy glass

How are we to believe? there is no scar
and every day ingrains
distrust of sight, of innocence –

Then love, moving in the mind's element,
shows again the clearness unbroken,
and all questions are at peace.

A deep-sea fisherman hauls up . . .

A deep-sea fisherman hauls up
a sprig of heather with bees upon it;

his coracle skims the top of a wood,
rides over a flowering meadow;

in that world contradiction is unknown,
resurrection has never been needed.

Starting out from the latitude of Byzantium . . .

Starting out from the latitude of Byzantium
Pytheas leaves that tideless world,
blue crystal globe –

Truth in the map's lighted circle cannot rival
regions of unshaken twilight, solid whirlwind,
rocks that wander invisible,
golden stone oozing from trees;

'The unknown must be there,' he murmurs;
'feel how it wrenches the known.'

Robert Kirk

He has been taken into his book,
out of ordinary time, the copy,
into the original;
and our world's end may leave him unscathed,
beyond harbour lights & human boundaries,
raking through shingle on the penultimate beach
for fossil unicorn.

Shadowless Air, Unchanging Season

Proserpina's garden, ropes of
        scarlet & leaden purple berries
as earth breathes in its dream,
        a snow-cold spring wells up through gravel,
            spreading into stillness
the rocks give off a heavy light
        thick as white honey

            And I have been
            all these things
            in clearings of a forest
            where Time is unknown

Valentine

All night
my heartbeat
scans your name

Along
the rivers
underground

Darkness
love's hidden
Pactolus

Holds in
deep caverns
the ripe sun

At night the snow is blue . . .

At night the snow is blue,
      reflecting a single eye,
waters above the firmament,
      colour that is alive.

Unravelling threads of rainbow
      return into the sun,
leaving a grey scratched mirror, now
      sealed like a stone.

Meaning has drained away as flood-water sinks into
      furrows,
Parchment & bone dangle creaking from a green gallows.

Wind-scattered leaves . . .

           wind-scattered leaves
remote as the gnarled | roots of the sea
as a heartbeat soft | & close & strange
a well where stars | all noonday shine
where the mind's eye | is slowly drowning
shadowless depth | swirls across the sand

[*Aeneid* vi]

Aeneid VI.4–901

His journey into death & prophecy
has taken, exactly, no time –

the cavern's eye blinks once
and he is back on the beach
    where the ships have not moved.

Remember
clear & still the sleeping shore
in these last moments before dawn,
before Aeneas can bring history.

Wyatt

Darkness like water has filled the hollow garden
where fragments of a drowned face float illegibly;
one yellowing elder tree hugs evil dreams;
this lake obeys no moon.

You learned the lessons of the moon
by heart, engraved on darkness;
shape-shifter, true to herself immortal.
Repeating 'But once I was' locks you into the past.

Do leaves imprinted in a jewel's past
live in her memory? Do you?
Take your tide into changefulness now,
from hands that offer bread –

                    and golden chains.

Seven Horizon Poems

I

Horizon means the thing you never reach,
but see, & long for, never touch;

dancing in a glittering net it parches
heart & eye & salt-wearied throat,

always an enchanted
telescope's range away –

like birds we peck at painted
varnished paper fruit

II

based on Fernando Pessoa

Far-off austere coastline
Leans to meet the ship coming in
With trees in which Distance has no share;
Nearer, the land opens in sounds & colours:
Disembark, and there are birds & flowers
Where, from afar, was only the abstract line.

All the possible shores have vanished; now
This is merely earth & water.

III

That cold colourless line,
seen once before, perhaps,
always almost remembered,
may hold lands that occupy no space,
may widen out into a crack that leads
to the true flower or tree
                or bird
                or fountain,
the last cape of this world,
Apollo's primeval orchard.

IV

A polished steel vizor
is the ship's horizon, a prison
that goes with us unchanging,
makes it hard to believe in movement,
mockery to believe our eyes.

V

translated from Lorenzo the Magnificent –
probably written in the 1480s

A wandering bird leaves its beloved shore
that has grown cold, and flies across the sea

. . . on every side waves, water, weariness,
nothing else to see, nothing else to feel,
no rock or branch to give a moment's rest

If a ship comes ploughing through the waters,
the sailors may be crueller than the storm . . .

I hover hesitating in this world

for when the mind has left its native land
confusion is the only thing it finds
and when it longs to seek for shores unknown
it ends in waves of doubt & weariness

VI

Palinurus, clawing at the cliff-side,
dragged by his heavy clothes,
numb & sick from the brine,
realises the god has not lied –
he is going to die on land:
the wreckers crunch towards him
                with their boat-hooks.

VII

Smeared with weeds & clay,
stung by sand & gravel,
Prometheus wades ashore
on to this island world,
carrying a precious thing –

brazier of rubies
            from ashes of sunrise,
tenderness in his great hands

that for our sake will be nailed to blackening rock.

Cranaë . . .

νήσῳ δ' ἐν Κραναῇ – ILIAD III

Cranaë,
      dark island
where first we lay
on warm grass
      & lavender,

                timeless, touches
                every moment,

colours every breath of common air.

To Thomas Cavalieri

Below the surface of raw stone
the hand's obedient eye can see
the shape that will grow into life
as the scales are prised away;

Snakes fray against a rock
to escape from their dying self
that quietly breaks & blows away,
emptied of colour & meaning;

And in your sudden sunlight
my old skin lies in heaps about your feet.

Uncollected Poems

One wing-beat of the heart . . .

One wing-beat of the heart can hold
centuries, heights of third heaven,
a stumble in a dream, a waking
lost in a small familiar field
within sight of the lights of home.

Coasting by a citadel . . .

Coasting by a citadel
time & the waves have picked clean,
you use the ancient gateway for a sea-mark;
over it watches that little statue,
like a shepherd with horns.
Centuries have ground the name away,
still brown-eyed Pan outlives
            Cassandra of the stone.

Outlawed by time, the cloud-land of Magonia . . .

Outlawed by time, the cloud-land of Magonia
sails on, silently;
the Fortunate Isles dodge in and out
of maps' reality;
he needs a harbour safe within him
who would sail that knowing sea.

Tarot VI

Yoked unequally, god-born & man
struggle to draw their swaying load,
one must give up, one cannot –
might Lazarus envy Stephen?

Hector is fated to lose all he can,
merely his human life, dying
for one form of the City
just before its destruction;

Aeneas to plunge many times
down where deep shadow swims,
between the dead and the future
to carry & transplant eternal Troy.

Sceilg Mhichíl

Your visible world is a sea-cave,
samphire, pale marshland jewelled with salt,
fog denying distance;
in solitude you watch icy rain
sieving away dead weeds,
wait for clouds to rise
from vast inner horizons
& green truths of faith
to grow on the rock.
Crossing earth's last river
will bring you no terror –
fear is already emptied, and all
fantastic dimensions of the universe
merely a dilapidated hut.

Et eius lucerna est desiderium

The whole flawless desert spirals inward,
crazily small & familiar-shaped
as a sharp-edged tooth
where time & again the dry tongue stumbles.

Bitter alchemy has reared these ramparts
called the dead to arms, guarding
an empty citadel;
they pace their dark rounds for ever
with grim unflickering lantern,
they have lost all song & memory
of light, of gardens beside the sea
where wind sprinkles brightness
and green boughs follow the shining tide.

Water-World

Cautiously paying out his life-line,
Memory the diver inches along leaden-footed,
through silence of the companionable drowned,
grazing incurious fish,
a rich clutter of relics.
One treasure or triviality raised
has to mean so many others
left embedded in blackness,
which the sea intends to keep.

Temenos

The reasons of all colour dwell in the sun,
where co-inherent rings of pure, heavy light
– white, crimson, gold – unfalteringly well up,
mark out the consecrated floor.

Swords interlinked form a rose or mirror,
catching a glint of their dance.

Draw near to this island in deep time.

Fill the air of the heart with a stillness of joy.

Margery Kempe

There is nothing against you
but the moon and seven stars.

Humble creature, God's will is your pathway.
Obeying him, you leave all that you know,
set out alone, give away what you need,
part from your companions –
trusting to meet them again
in all men's kindly country.

There is nothing against you
but the moon and seven stars.

Sunset pours
through the western rose-window
as omnipotent grace wells glowing
through the stony world –
till all are brought safe home:
knowing this, you will never fear
the moon and seven stars.

Needed on Voyage

This icon, these creatures are a door of hope
through which we pray to the Unimaged
in whose light we shall come to realise
'all these belonged to the world of image',
as they drift away, having done their work –
as the Sibyl's face fades from the moon,
and mummified, the worn-out sun
is thrown into a dusty corner.

Marculf

Saturn, wolf of the boundary,
prowls in unchanging twilight
where this world's knowledge falters and fails,
our loves and learning cannot breathe;
he is lord of a country
'where no man may step with feet',
controls the unseen watchers
whom we sense, of a sudden, in panic,
when they pierce our unshaken air.

Metamorphoses

Sharply made creature of a strange element,
past the barrier before thinking of it,
Glaucos looks back, a moment,
to the life he cannot quite remember, where
dead fish danced joyously on the green salt-grass;
he licked it, in wonder, and became a god of the sea.

Shorn of his flames, Apollo
dwells in secret below the long rocks,
passes through the pools of autumn,
every year transmuted
from gold to black, and returning
from burial to springtime.

A building may haunt a place where once it stood,
be seen at shifting times, by one eye and not another.
A solid, visible door lets you in –
outside time slips awry for a moment,
and the house has vanished with its captive.

II

Temple in a green field by the river,
apple trees, oaks and wells,
you let through some splintered light
                    into our day
from other places whose myths you are.

Metallic moonlight sprinkles
the golden bird in his garden,
icy fire naked of cloud
glints on the blindness of a jewelled eye.

When the mouth of night opens,
hillside and hieroglyph pour away;
where no moon has ever shone
something lost and crying
                              blunders about
trying to find a way back in.

The snow is waiting to be scribbled on . . .

The snow is waiting to be scribbled on
– beasts write cursive, birds leave runes –
and earth, much whiter than the sky,
brims with light, like a full moon,
having received abundance.

Memory is a palimpsest, worm-eaten, speckled;
the trivial text is clear, the good corrupted
– or some years completely vanished
when the birds of Rhiannon sang –
still both worlds huddle darkly side by side.

Easter '87

Man imagines escaping at last
from the kingdom of idols,
but the tracks lead again and again
back to the ivory gate.

Ash & salt & quiet sand
petrify one rippling
meadow after another;
a sickness devours the stone.

Healing light overflows from an empty grave;
God's body is a crystal; whole or broken,
every part of the crystal is full of sun.

Corinna

Her plaited hair like a garland of wheat,
her grace a sensible frugality,
Corinna scattered her seed-poems
a handful at a time.
In their world, stream & mountain
are tousled immortals
who sing before the court of gods
& speak with oracles, all
harmoniously linked:
the river's daughters marry
divine sea and sky,
to bear a race of heroes;
poets adorn & unfold their myths,
the austere shape of beauty.

Snake

Flows like a river but is solid
warm flesh & bone;
cold flint eye, never blinks;
patiently grows plump within the backbone
of man's buried ancestors,
on rich marrow of oracular wisdom
– for now they are dead they know everything.

Poisoned the heel of our mother Eurydice,
the mind of our mother Eve;
lay crushed and cracked apart by our mother Mary;
tanist of the waning year,
he struggles forever with his equally
cruel king, the shining Eagle
– do we envy his knowledge
                         or his knowingness?

Lovingly the trees follow Orpheus . . .

Lovingly the trees follow Orpheus,
quietly sit to hear him sing,
in rings round his rough throne,
as Merlin's incantation
brought Stonehenge across the sea.
Each marks out his clearing,
walled in by magic air,
which will never vanish completely
though all the landscape alters.

On what are now open downs appear
ghostly woods or rock,
living on one heartbeat of that song.

Easter '88

The stone sky has been rolled away
so that we can look inside,
Eve's evergreen tree is felled at last,
and bodies of buried saints
                              people the living town.

We see him in front of us, walking, plain,
                              closer than bird or star,
towards the lakeside in his own country,
                              and the wonderful salmon,
                                        and bread . . .

The incredible happening so lightly
made us able to receive that simple dawn.

This end of the bridge you can see . . .

This end of the bridge you can see
by the light of lamps like berries
of giant mistletoe;
its grey road splits into long red paths
of sunset that burn on the bridge's brow
and make a soft floating darkness
dance round your eye,

rays from that rich hearth
drawing its children home.

The dead ring of winter . . .

The dead ring of winter settles down,
            and fits exactly.
But our heavy dark-blue chain
            will rust away,
The cold snake burst
            into a scatter of tiny ribs.
Under deepest ice there lives,
            bruised and blackened,
            running water.

N-Town, _c._ 1500

(after the plays)

'iv pair of angels' wings, iv diadems, vi golden skins',
writes the clerk, among items for beer
and hay and carpenters' wages;

'For mending the devils' coats'
(they fight and somersault in the street
more furiously every summer, or singe themselves
in their capering; which reminds me,) 'for painting of hell mouth.'

'For half a yard of Red Sea'
(they seem to think painted canvas lasts for ever,
but it will crack & flake when jerked about
and trampled on); 'Payd for a pair of gloves for God'
(he said he'd lost them, but he gave them to a wench
in my opinion.)

'For the Spirit of God's coat'
(how can he contrive to tear it, when all he has to do
is to stand still and bless the Disciples?) 'a coat
with hosen and tayle for the Serpente'
(at least I can see how his gets worn out);
'dinners for the angel
and pendon bearer' (good lad, that angel,
but eats like a famishing wodwose; at last, the
bottom of the page:)

'for setting the world on fire v^{d}.'
(Deo Gratias, for another year.)

Initiation

A smoky lantern swinging in a tree
lights and clouds the dancer
who honours a small unwinking beast
sent from the Man in Black
to obey her in all harm.

Greedy, fastidious, the familiar devours
his adoring possessor;
his price is a life's blood.
Speck of slime or fur, he will overshadow her
huge as a haunted mountain,
will hollow her out and leave
at last not even corruption
but a dumb dry shell fit only to be burned.

First Mystery

She who is to be
God's garden
waits at the heart of stillness.
All paths have led to this moment.

The angel bows before humility
and innocence
in their house of gold,
their power to change all worlds.

Between them on the lily's boughs
a man hangs crucified.

Paths & bushes have their own dance . . .

Paths & bushes have their own dance
in this wicked light,
shift without moving
like shapes in twilit water;
along eternity's figure-of-eight
dead and living man alternate
like a shadow and its tree.

This wood has many centres:
one is hidden and defended
by knotted rock & thorn,
the garden so old and so new
where all our fragments are gathered,
and neither *healed* nor *mended*, but made
as they were before Adam's time,

Adam the Namer and Wrecker.

Mercury to the Alchemist

All our secrets of one Image must spring
(RIPLEY)

Out of the tomb you fetch my shape.

You think I am dark Lazarus
in need of your fountain.

You would shrink me to a narrow singleness,
cut my wings, because you cannot fathom
the changes of dance between the worlds;

but your broadest heaven is only winter arches,
and what you grasp is a wraith

in a mask of smoke; I weave no treachery.

As writing read in a dream . . .

As writing read in a dream,
remembered in clarity
and urgent importance
till the eyes open,
dwindles then like foam;
as hedge birds feel
coolness dawn along their bones
an hour before the light;
so poet and prophet
must know how to wait,
how to recognise.

II

Nightmare's dark lantern
flickers, revealing
from dead forest or ragged cavern
a glint of eyes like stones,
in wait for the traveller who strays.

Such fear is needful
as inexorable
– poets have always known it to be
tanist and twin of true
vision, brightness beyond reason.

Fisher King

We need no movement in this place,
being centred upon our own Hallows,
ringed by their unchanging procession.

Cut off from the City of men,
in my castle outside time
I await my deliverer.

But the icy bright vision returns,
wounds with precision & subtlety,
dead on the scar;

small are the islands of light.

Instructions for the Orphic Initiate Soul

(3rd or 4th cent. BC)

You will find on the left of Hades' House a fountain,
and beside it standing a white cypress.
Come not near this fountain.
And you will find another of cold water flowing
from Memory's lake. It is guarded.
Say, 'I am child of earth and starry heaven,
but my breed is heavenly – this you know.
I am parched with thirst and dying; give me quickly
cold water flowing from Memory's lake.'
And they will give you to drink from the holy fountain,
and you will rule among the other blessed heroes . . .

Stars are pollen of that blue tree . . .

Stars are pollen of that blue tree
                the night sky

Its leaves make the noise of rain

Scattered gleams float down,
                scales of its bark,

and here the dust is bright.

Epithalamion

To golden Sardis Anaktoria will bring
her moonlight to outshine
                its court of dancing stars;
to golden Sardis Anaktoria will bring
her loveliness, and leave us
                blind in her eclipse.
Here autumn veins the air, as quartz lies in dark rock,
and swallows leave this chill
                to seek their glowing land.

No More Sea

Beyond the mirror's inmost horizon
a crack will open, and all its people
– their slavery broken, apes no longer –
will march upon their ancient boundary,
re-cross Lethe, return to that Memory
in whose full pity are recognised all
deep-drowned faces in green water.

Sunt aliquid Manes

The stone door opens once a year
and in roaring silence
they stream upward and scatter,
opal eyes blank,
over our dark living world.

Even Cerberus wanders unchained
in this night.

Here a candle weeps its winding-sheet
or a beast knows they draw near –

let them eat their food and return in peace.

Return of a Dead Lady

Sleepwalking back
      along the repetitious columned road
over dark plains uncannily empty
      of expected fiend or ambush
lead me to those living strangers
      to whom you say I once belonged –

yet I have never known anything
      but quietly pacing this path
in the chill thin light after sunset;
      I have always been dead.
A rainy moon has blurred my sight;
      no sound or memory can break my rest,
private as a jewel beneath the mountain.

Approaching night's boundary, Hermes must fail me
      and I go on alone;
      those who have called me, do they know
I shall never leave them again?

Fortuna

Set in glory, a white rose within the sun,
golden-wristed icon, Solomon
wields ring & sceptre that enchain
demons who cloak the air like sandstorms
& tiny squinting atoms of malice
to a like obedience.

> [*After his death, the devils continued long in deceived
> servility, until worms gnawing through the staff he
> leaned on brought the dead man toppling down and
> broke his final shape of domination.*]

Asmodeus accuser black as coal,
ruler of a nameless country, bides below,
tranquil-smiling, for the wheel to turn –
only his torn & gilded claws
recall he once was el dorado
set in glory, a white rose within the sun.

Facilis descensus

Under your darkness without hope of dawn
tangled the living lie, Master;

enchanted by the huge simplicity
of abdication, they renounced the sun.

No-one need learn | the black paternoster,
all know it; he asks | mere acknowledgement.

He moulds them with oppression they first chose,
as nightmare rides each will
                              once offered joyously –

all is not harvest & the witch is never dead.

Tarot IX

Enclosed within a room, a pentacle, a crystal,
on his mind's island
Prospero labours, travelling
down through jade-green caves among roots of the sea,
veins of ruby, moss-agate fronds
                    or opals' fire.

His lantern illumines inner places
of his own Adam earth
where elements ripen & another zodiac turns;
his own sun and moon determine wars,
himself the first victim
                    and victory.

Through creation with rejection, spiralling paradox,
he approaches the Stone, the end of longing,
hidden below his darkness.

Gorre

Silently the hidden house
waits among apple trees
ringed by rampart, hedge and stream;
music of the silver branch
had locked all gates, corroded keys
and drowned the bridge
so that summer can never escape.
She may not age who remains here,
bride of the cloud-faced king;
Guenever dreams the return of human time,
noise, imperfection, change,
that will shatter the wall of air
when her wounded rescuer comes to her
and brightness floods in on the tide.

Gloss on *Vita Brendani*

Seeking a desert in the ocean,
destined place of each one's resurrection,
holy kingly in their scarred leathery skin,
richly feasted on wild root and leaf,
drop the oars overboard when land lies behind them
too far to be seen,
and all God's will ahead –
every passion in a single obedience
offered to the secret journey,
pattern of that last one
whose beginning only is known.

For Peter

A flat gold face floating
smiles calmly out of its elder world
secure in remoteness,
chill as the crystal belfry of a star.
This icon says, The King is here,
this presence is his power;
look into his wide eyes,
dazzled open with omnipotent light;
gaze out of the dragon-world of rivers underground,
from iron-forest where nightmare walks,
from the marsh where treasures rot
or the race of white water,
here broods unchanging the shadow of God.

Carnac

Strings of menhirs race across a windy field
and their dark builders lie in quietness;
cosy as an egg their treasure hides,
flint, bronze, blue beads like eyes,
ploughed over unseen by returning seasons;
even their naked name is lost.
They remain, cold as a moon-rainbow,
private as paintings in a tomb,
but like you having borne in their bodies,
once, it may be, a dead dream,
having known thirst for a living spring,
fear of that triumphant skeleton.

Awake before dawn . . .

Awake before dawn, still
        deep in the waters of night
Stone awaits unmoved
        awareness of being stone.

Through faintly ebbing dark uncurl
Tendril, tentacle, fin,
As the world begins.

The moon's net, pouring with light,
Hauls blue scorpion, wolf & ape to land,
Chained in her squinting rays;

Millennia pass,
        a sparrow cheeps,
man in his iron crown travels into day.

Revenant

So changed that even my bones are new
despite myself I am come home;
all I left you last time
was black sinew and rivelled skin –
no danger of being remembered.
I could pick out which shield I bore at Troy,
(all the tricks, if you wanted)
spin travelling soul's tales to daze your heart;
yet you could never help me find
my centre of the winds' turning rose,
impossible Ithaca.

Those gates have long been locked . . .

Those gates have long been locked, their keys
rusted into one red clod;
around the borders drift
uneasy shapes in deepening cloud.

Rain and wind unravel patiently
back to sterile sand
that private land we once created,
& have casually forgotten.

Hero

Gash the stone, strike blood from the wind,
wrestle down the swollen lumbering dead,
ride the sleet-storm of nightmare;
all miracles are allowed you for a little time,

until the moment when you forget
one detail, turn to an unlucky side,
fail to answer beggar or cripple, taste forbidden meat . . .
the hawk stoops & your clear sky splinters,
worm in the bone's core rejoices

you have followed your path so truly
there can be no escape.

As light flows deep . . .

As light flows deep within darkness,
night into the gold eye of day,
so your heart's mind enters mine,
strolls among the pools & fruit trees,
lapis lazuli and crocus,
reads the verses that grow there.

Mnesarchides

On a vine-shaded terrace above the sea
where tiny suns flicker
innumerable as plankton,
ephemeral as foam,
Pythagoras dreams of knowing
all his origins:

'I have been, I have been . . .
can the phoenix remember
earlier phoenix it has been?
I have been a herald between the worlds, like my father
    Mercury;
Menelaus killed me at Troy;
I have been a wandering prophet's ghost,
and a fisherman still as a rock;
were they all reflections from one light, so,
scattered throughout leaf & wave, longing always
to return
to their silent fountain?'

Love makes the crystal . . .

Love makes the crystal
deep for divination,
links words like dew on spider's thread
that will describe one day truly
green bud, green flower, as they grow
on river-banks of the moon.

Ruffling the field's uneasy fur . . .

'It is very near us that country is, it is on
every side; it may be on the bare
hill behind it is, or it may be in the
heart of the wood.'

Ruffling the field's uneasy fur,
the wind
makes itself visible.

One feather dropped by phoenix,
giving light from within,
revealed sunrise.

Your desire creates me, calls me up
from the drowned world, transforming
drops of dark salt into diamond.

Heroic tombs facing the sea . . .

Heroic tombs facing the sea,
worm-eaten rock, shape-shifters,
dare still & out-stare
invaders through the mist
that rings Man's island;

not wise the thought of Weland's bones,
a resting-place for Arthur
or for the Noble Head:
for Merlin's garden there are greater,
invisible, protectors whom no grave could hold.

Where the cloud of colour . . .

Where the cloud of colour
touches our horizon
a rose of roads opens,
a sheaf of light suddenly unbound;

nacreous gleam a fingertip can stroke
guards a depth of remoteness
that is tranquil for ever
– beyond all explaining

love's dove descending
before the rainbow fades
& while the shell endures.

Tidal waves of light . . .

Tidal waves of light
            burst over bare branches;
autumn's buds
            are stained by the spindrift,
gold is concentrated into green:
'So death doth touch the Resurrection.'

Out from the moon's dark hillside . . .

Out from the moon's dark hillside
ghosts drift across our noon-day,
chill the April sun,
rap on windows of dream.
They are forgetting how they ever lived
under this darkness.

And I can scarcely recognise
grief, now levelled by the tide
invading upland gardens,
the fierce immortal sea.

Tonn Tuili

Flood-wave returns
and the island comes alive, like a ship;
movement of time returns,
& flickering light;
banks of snow and sand
melt in a moment,
no longer lying.

Poplars delicately paint themselves . . .

Poplars delicately paint themselves
in the green river

I am your stream
lying close in your shade

This cannot be a dream, because
in dreams we never see the sun.

Rilke

Even if we know love's landscape
and the little churchyard with its mourning names,
and the frighteningly silent ravine for which others are bound,
time & again we walk together under ancient trees,
time & again lie down among flowers
opposite the sky.

Long streaming waves unfurl . . .

Long streaming waves unfurl
through my blood's Mediterranean
– love has taught it tides.

The timelessness of being in love . . .

The timelessness of being in love
brings closer
lands never wholly lost
beneath that   bitter wave,

       alchemically transformed
       into time aorist.

To Lucretius

Longing to clear our mind of gods
you show them far away in depths of light
unsounded, unmoved by our thunderstorms & nightmares,
and teach us to repeat *They do not care, they cannot care;*
yet you never scratch the crystal of that older vision,
world of green moss & rocks where the cool stream
was a girl, of silent places among hills
where a man might hear the Muses breathing,
when Venus linked loving bodies in shady woods,
and Summanus walked the temples of the calm night sky.

I love you like a small tidal river . . .

Venit amor subitaque animum dulcedine movit.

I love you like a small tidal river
giving itself to sea when the strong tide turns.

Indivisible the soaking sand below the water's boundary,
each the other's fullness, mingled
frankincense & phoenix ash.

Shingle clatters down the slope
obeying one endless undertow,
the brute magnet of the moon.

Lie gently in your natural harbour,
my bones the breakwater, your heart
the moon's reflection;
tears divide light into colours,
emeralds
           through the fine rain.

Where scattered bones of snow lay, long ago,
ripe unbroken fruit
                rests in the tall grass.

'They say the real Jack-in-the-Green
comes back once in a hundred years'

A dancing orchard green & gold, ghost of Dionysos,
Jack jingles through the village where dust glitters like
    gems
as 'nowhere' becomes 'now here'
                   and Greensleeves the new season
turns into Ceridwen through all kingdoms of the creatures
shape-changing forever round the sorrowful starry wheel.

Heredia, Propertius

The ruined temple stands on the headland
And Death has mingled in the tawny earth
Goddesses of marble with bronze heroes,
Their glory buried in the lonely grass.

– And Veii was a kingdom long ago
And in the forum stood a golden throne
But now the sullen shepherd blows his horn
Within its walls, & crops grow from its bones.

The One-Strand River

Little heart-shaped footmarks
inscribe on dark water
a trail of stars

beyond Styx
but not beyond Lethe

(Hate having two banks
can be crossed & left behind)

Ghostly rock overshades . . .

Ghostly rock overshades this neat ploughed field,
embroidered with silver weeds & roses
fed on the salts of a vanished ocean.
        Merlin having seen it before
        knows he will see it again.

Every facet of the starry flint
may have planets of its own; waves of percussion
open & glitter; the stone is made of air.
        Merlin foreknows his dungeon; the air
        will be a black stone over him.

Our slow magic . . .

Our slow magic
          turns hours of longing
into drops of molten gold

Osiris and Hippolytus
          are sown in the furrows
where all mythologies are true,

the magical invocation,
          the wall of water,
unbroken.

'You pattern of all those'

The sun swims along glittering veins
          underground,
his gift imperial dark red streams,
          blood of earth.

He is a storm-lantern pale as mistletoe
          on the mast
sailing up to the doorway of night's beehive tomb
          facing east.

To the wanderer scorched by salt among phantom trees
          he will bring
taste of earth & grit & water alive
          beneath snow.

Amethyst light of ocean's heart . . .

Amethyst light of ocean's heart
breathes in deep secret here,
below all words for storm.

Everlasting the fall, higher and higher,
into temples of the midnight sky,
beyond all words for loss or return.

In this language . . .

In this language
voice and song are the same word
richness is not merely brocade
sunrise awakens rivers
of gems under the earth

In this language
all maps are journeys of delight
lamps like mistletoe berries burn
at this end of twilight's bridge
& make a soft darkness
float about the eye

like a glittering fish in his element
love dwells
in this language

Love lying close as a heartbeat . . .

Love lying close as a heartbeat
learns at last the word give,
soft & vulnerable in your hand
where trees bearing crescent moonstones
make winter arches.

Orpheus among Elysian willows . . .

(Pausanias X.30)

Orpheus among Elysian willows
passes through the sleep of many lives,
able now to gaze down a fathomless road,
a glassy curve
                that never ends,
a wave unbroken.

Taliesin flees through changing shapes,
appears from the dark ocean –
now I am come here
                to the remnant of Troia –

all may have made the voyage,
                one alone remembers.

Ice-needles prickle on the skin . . .

Ice-needles prickle on the skin
of poet's or magician's mind
long before exhausted watchmen
crouched on a stony roof in frost & dewfall
see blaze up like daylight
the messenger all can see.

Proleptic thought
replaces time, as the radiant Stone
will ripen imperfect metal,
may go so far that we awake,
stranded, on a dry beach after the future.

Day, blank floodwater, drains away . . .

Day, blank floodwater, drains away
          into the forest floor of sleep,
tasting of blackened leaves –
                    but here
all night
          my heartbeat
                    scans your name.

The blackbird hammers arabesques . . .

The blackbird hammers arabesques

       of silver wire
into day's opaque metal,

sprinkles glittering ashes

       of Hermes' tree
over waters of darkness.

'My mind does that when I think about you'

Flung from their splintered ship,
heavy with salt & slashed by flint
they collapse on a hard-hearted land,
painfully build a fire among her rocks;
as they are gasping in saw-edged air
the specular stone melts,
      the fields of Neptune
          bear vitrified gold.

New Grange

Enter . . .

whirling suns resound
        engraved on the threshold,
flowers of immortal fire
        shake their sistra.

In a dark school you will overcome
        the colour of mortality

when a far-off clarity seems near.

Translations

Sophocles' *Ajax*, 646 ff.

Enormous time that will not be numbered
brings the hidden to light and the clear into darkness.
Nothing is fixed beyond hope of change;
the fearsome oath, the hardened resolve,
give way. I that was hard as brittle steel
am tempered now by a woman's words.
I pity her, I cannot leave her widowed,
with an orphan son, among enemies.
I will go the sea-meadows, and in holy waters
become pure again and escape Athene's anger,
I will find a solitary place
and bury this my evil sword, never to be seen again,
where Night and Hell will hold it . . .

Go in, girl, and pray to the gods,
pray they will grant me all my heart's desire.
And you, friends, do me so much honour,
tell Teucer, when he comes, to take care of me
and be kind to you, for I have a journey to go;
do what I ask, and soon you may hear,
although I am wretched now, that I have come safe home.

Wind, wind of the sea,
carrying the quick ships
over the waves' flood,
where will you take
me with my sorrow?
Whose house will receive me,
sold into slavery?
Is my harbour in Doris
or in Phthia, richly watered
by Apidanos, father
of sweetest rivers?
Will oars that sweep the sea
bring me to an island,
to lead a wretched life
between four walls?
To Dēlos where the palm-tree was born,
mingling its holy branches with laurel
to honour god's birth?
Shall I join the Delians, praising
Artemis' hair tied back with gold
and her hunting bow?
In the city of Athēnē,
shall I embroider
on her crocus-yellow cloak
young horses yoked together
on a flowery woven field?
Or figures of Titans
laid low by Zeus
with the lightning fire?
Oh my poor children,
my parents, my country
smouldering in ruin,
smashed by spears —

and myself a slave
in a strange land now,
having left Asia
for Europe,
the marriage-bed of Death.

[*Euripides*]

Five Poems from *The Greek Anthology*

On this her daughter's tomb
                    Cleina could not stop
crying bitterly for her short-lived child,
calling to the soul of Philaenis, who crossed
Death's pale joyless river before her wedding day.

[*Anyte*]

Throwing her arms around her father,
her eyes streaming with pale tears,
Erato spoke these last words:
'Oh father, I am leaving you; over my eyes
Death draws his darkness –
                    and I go into the dark.'

[*Anyte*]

The child Myro made this tomb
for her grasshopper, a field-nightingale,
and her cicada that lived in the trees,
and she cried because pitiless Death
had taken both of her friends.

[*Anyte*]

Melinna herself! It *is* – see how kindly
her gentle face looks down at me,
& how like her mother she is!
It's good when children look so like their parents.

[*Nossis*]

This is Thaumareta's picture, and how well it captures
her elegance, her mild-eyed beauty!
If your little watch-dog saw you here,
she'd wag her tail, believing you were her mistress.

[*Nossis*]

Eirenaios, ἀγκὰς ἑλοῦσά μ' ἔχεις

Dans tes bras, dans ton lit, tu me tiens sur toi
    enchaîné, je ne veux point de liberté;
L'âme et les corps tout enchevêtrés
    voguent à la dérive au gré des courants de l'amour.

Rhea Silvia's Dream

translated from Ennius, written c. 200 BC

In my dream a beautiful man
led me away through groves of willow
by river banks
to strange places; and then
I was wandering there alone,
lagging behind, looking for you . . .

but you were not in my heart
and the path
         would not keep still . . .

Turning our backs on sunlight . . .

Turning our backs on sunlight & the day,
beyond all frontiers of the world we know
exiled, we dare to cross forbidden darkness
to evening's edge on the last far shore.
Our ships venture into the Ocean
that bears ghastly monsters beneath its heavy waves,
sea-brutes like dogs, that try to climb aboard.
The sound thickens our fear; the tide
suddenly deserts us, and the fleet
lies helpless on a sandbank, prey
to beasts that will rip & smash.
One man on the prow tries in vain
to burst through that blinding air,
but the world has been torn away; he gasps,
'Where is it taking us? Time & space have escaped;
this is nature's closed, everlasting dark.
Can we find another world, untouched, out there,
or people under another heaven?
The gods call us back, for mortal eyes
may not look upon the end of all things.
Our oars must not disturb these eerie waters;
how dare we break the stillness of the gods?'

[*'Iam pridem post terga diem solemque relictum . . .'* –
anonymous Roman on Germanicus' North Sea expedition,
c. 16 AD]

The Milky Way

In dark-blue heaven a white road shines
like a sunrise opening the sky,
like a path dividing two green fields,
worn by cart-wheels repeating their journey;
as a ship draws her furrow on the sea,
printing on the white water a road
that unwinds from a coiling whirlpool,
this frontier of the dark height glows,
& splits with light the dark-blue heaven.

[*Manilius, Book I*]

'Come uccel peregrin che il lito amato . . .'

A wandering bird leaves its beloved shore
that has grown cold, and flies across the sea;

. . . on every side waves, water, weariness,
nothing else to see, nothing else to feel,
no rock or branch to give a moment's rest.
If a ship comes ploughing through the waters,
the sailors may be crueller than the storm . . .

I hover hesitating in this world

for when the mind has left its native land
confusion is the only thing it finds
and when it longs to seek for shores unknown
it ends in waves of doubt & weariness.

Petrarca, 'A qualunque animale'

For every beast that lives on earth
(except the few that hate the sun)
the time in which he labours is the day;
but when the sky lights up its stars'
one seeks his shed, one his home in the wood,
to rest at least until the dawn.

And I, as soon as the fair dawn
begins to shatter shadow round the earth,
awaking animals in every wood,
must with my sighs accompany the sun;
then when I see the flaming stars,
I weep and long again for day.

When evening chases out bright day
and here our darkness makes another's dawn,
thoughtfully I gaze on cruel stars
who moulded me from feeling earth,
and curse the day I saw the sun,
that makes me like a wild man from the wood.

Never, I think, in any wood
so rough a beast has lived, by night or day,
as this one whom I mourn in shade and sun,
and never cease, in evening or at dawn;
although my mortal body is of earth,
my firm desire comes from the stars.

Before I return to the glowing stars
or fall into the lovers' wood,
leaving my body to make dusty earth,
might I see pity in her, just one day
that might restore whole years; before the dawn
might I grow rich, after the set of sun.

Night I be with her when the weary sun
has set and we see nothing but the stars,
one night alone, but one without a dawn,
and she not turn into a leafy wood
escaping from my arms, as on that day
when Phoebus followed her on earth.

But I shall be under earth within dry wood,
and day will be set full of tiny stars,
before so sweet a dawn will join the sun.

Vittoria Colonna, 'A che sempre chiamar la sorda morte'

What use to shout in Death's deaf ears
and make heaven compassionate with crying,
if I can clip this great desire's wings
myself, and free my heart from grief?
It would be better than begging mercy
from closed doors, to open one to forgetting
and close the other on thinking,
to conquer both myself and cruel Fate.
All schemes and ways my soul invents
to escape this pain's blind prison
I have tried, and all in vain.
The only thing now is to discover
whether I have enough sense to turn
this mad, hopeless longing to better things.

Visitation Poem

Lope de Vega, a la Virgen

Joyful
Mysteries

- O where are you going,
  alone on the mountain?
- I fear not the night,
  for I carry the sun.
- O where are you going,
  with God as your husband,
  O glorious mother
  of God your creator?
  O what will you do
  if the day draws to evening
  and night overtakes you
  alone on the mountain?
- I fear not the night,
  for I carry the sun.
- I look at the stars
  and they bring back my sadness,
  but your eyes are shining
  & brighter by far.
  The stars & the darkness
  are rising before us,
  the daylight is hidden
  away from your face.
- I fear not the night,
  for I carry the sun.

Another
Visitation Poem

see also

"The day Our Lady full of
christ entered the door-
ard of 'her relative"

Notes

Amy must have
thought the words
"ROW HEATH" —
denoted some sort
of RETAIL PARK —
that she could go
shopping in with a
CREDIT CARD — i.e.
MY CREDIT CARD
THAT SHE HAD
ALDREADY STOLEN

Notes

Two of Sally Purcell's books contained notes, which are given here first. In my notes which follow, I have confined myself to notes on the text, most of which come from comparing printed and mss. versions. A commentary could be written on the poems, although most of the references are easily traced.

Dark of Day

64 *Ars Longa*: Flamel was a fourteenth-century Parisian scribe and bookseller who turned alchemist in his old age and achieved the Magnum Opus.

71 *At South Leigh*: the church of South Leigh in Oxfordshire has a wall-painting of St Michael weighing a soul; on one side devils try to pull it down, and on the other Our Lady stands, representing the Doctrine of Exchange or Substitution, the co-inherence of all souls whereby they contribute to each other's salvation (*Arthurian Torso*, pp. 123, 143), and the Atonement.

72 *For a Wilderness*: the warrior Angatyr's sword was buried with him, and the only person who could retrieve it was his daughter Hervör (it had to be a man's son usually, but Angatyr had no sons); she succeeded, in spite of the attempts of the dead in the other burial-mounds to prevent her. Such magic swords would not go with any but the next closest representative of the family after their master's death.

86 *Woodchester*: at Woodchester in Gloucestershire is a magnificent fourth-century mosaic pavement of Orpheus surrounded by beasts and birds, which is only uncovered about once in ten years, because it lies under the churchyard.

145   *Celyddon*: the magic shape-melting wood that is the northern boundary of this world; see also the marvellous line by Alun Lewis, 'Or Celidon the hollow forest called'.

147   *'And you shall find all true but the wild Iland'*: from Beaumont and Fletcher's *The Maid's Tragedy*, II.ii.73.

148   *'and a song I tell to no man . . .'*: from the anonymous sixteenth-century Spanish *Romance del infante Arnaldos*; reference to A. E. Housman, *More Poems* 45.

150   *Dr Dee* (1527–1608): astrologer, magician and mathematician.

151   *Linquenda tellus*: 'You will have to leave the land you love . . .', Horace, *Odes*, II.14.

152   *Tomis*: the grim place on the Black Sea to which Ovid was banished; much use of *Tristia* III.

155   *Crinagoras*: from *Palatine Anthology* VI.253.

156   *Elizabeth of Bohemia*: daughter of James I, who was married to the Elector Palatine in 1613, and as part of whose wedding festivities *The Tempest* was probably first performed. The poem refers to a strange and sinister-looking engraving in Frances Yates' book *The Rosicrucian Enlightenment*.

162   *Amairgen*: poet who uttered the first poem spoken in Ireland. See A. and B. Rees, *Celtic Heritage* (Thames and Hudson, London, 1961) p. 98.

165   *Robert Kirk* (?1664–92?): a Scots Gaelic-speaking minister who wrote *The Secret Commonwealth of Elves, Fauns and Fairies* (*c.* 1691) about the Good People and their world, and the times it touches ours. As Yeats says, 'It is very near us that country is, it is on every side; it may be on the bare hill behind it is, or it may be in the heart of the wood.' The best edition is *The Secret Commonwealth*, ed. Stewart Sanderson (D.S. Brewer, The Folklore Society, Cambridge & Ipswich, 1976).

166   *Pactolus*: the river in which Midas washed himself, its sands in consequence turning to gold.

174   *Cranaë*: where Paris and Helen stopped on the first evening of their flight (*Iliad* III.445); see also the end of Patrick Leigh Fermor's book, *Mani* (John Murray, London, 1950).

174   *Thomas Cavalieri*: Michaelangelo's last *inamorato*.

Editor's Notes

By the Clear Fountain

Four poems in this booklet were reprinted in *Lake & Labyrinth*:
'Born between wood and water . . .', 'Lancelot at Almesbury',
'Lament for Yonec' and 'From Euripides, *Troades* 1060 ff.'. They
are omitted here and left in place in the later collection.

91   *Our blood is a red coral . . .*: the poem has a footnote 'written
at Knossos 1979'.

93   *Surfaces*: I have used a typescript instead of the version in
By the Clear Fountain. It cuts an opening paragraph:

> Ice lies upon the river's tomb,
> its alabaster effigy
> covering busy corruption;

95   *Ted's*: the Duke of Cambridge, a pub in Little Clarendon
Street, Oxford. It is now closed.

Guenever and the Looking Glass

'Dr Dee (ii)' is omitted and given its place in *Lake & Labyrinth*.

101   *Guenever and the Looking-Glass*: a ms. version has 'bright-
ness' for 'the brightness' in line 6, and 'kill, or dazzle,' for
'kill, dazzle,' in line 9.

103   *Mermaid*: in line 2 I preferred the ms. reading to that of the
text in *Guenever and the Looking Glass*, 'streamed fluttering
around her in air'.

106   *Views of Loss*: I have used the typescript version. The text
in *Guenever and the Looking Glass* reads at line 4 'as a bird's';
line 7, 'through tranquil, treasure-paved sea-light.'; 8,
'meteorite'; 9, 'black-faced comet' (without the article);
lines 7 and 9 are indented.

107   *A crown of iron & reddening bone*: in the penultimate line I
preferred the ms. version of 'flame' for 'flare'.

110   *Loquitur spiritus*: a ms. is dated 20/iii/78.

Lake and Labyrinth

115   *Lancelot at Almesbury*: in *By the Clear Fountain*, the poem had a separate first stanza:

> Helayne died years ago,
> mother of holy Galahad my son,
> and took the ebbing tide down to her grave
> in Arthur's royal city.

I have given the version from *Lake & Labyrinth*, which is also in a more recent ms., though its first two lines are obscure. The lineation of the ending is also changed.

118   *Dedication*: headed '(dedication, to Alasdair)' in a ms.

121   *'I see them walking in an Air of glory'*: I have used the later typescript version which has minor changes.

122   *From Caelica LXXXVII, The Eternal Glasse*: this is a revised version of the text in *Lake & Labyrinth*, which mentions only Fulke Greville, not his work, in the title. That earlier version also reads in line 3 'the earth'; in line 7 'of inexorable surface' and line 9 has a comma at the end.

141   *From Euripides*, Troades *1060 ff.*: I have re-inserted the third line, 'altar and lantern freeze', which is in *By the Clear Fountain* and a typescript but is missing from the text in *Lake & Labyrinth*.

142   *St Columcille*: a typescript version has for the last line 'craze this day with lightning, day with dreams.', but this repetition of 'day' must be a typing error.

Fossil Unicorn

145   *Easter '84*: I have added the year back into the title from ms., as there are other dated Easter poems.

146   *Receding into mist . . .*: entitled 'To R.J.P.' in ms.

149   *Out from time's tumulus . . .*: this is entitled 'For Advent' in a typescript version, which has 'wavers, ebbs & returns,' at line 6. The *Fossil Unicorn* manuscript has 'waves', which may be a slip of the hand, although it survived into print.

150   *Dr Dee* (IV): a ms. version has a space before the last line.

151   *Moor, mound & crag . . .*: a ms. version has the epigraph: 'where was it that I went /So unencumbered? (R. Graves)'.

161 *Sestina for Two Voices*: a ms. is dated 31/xii/92. I have restored from the *Fossil Unicorn* ms. the dashes which indicate speakers.

167 *At night the snow is blue* . . .: on a ms. version, where the text is identical but the layout is changed, the poem is dated 5/3/1995, and a title 'The One and the Many' with its ascription to Yeats is pencilled in. There is also another ms. version with the poem as three quatrains.

167 *Wind-scattered leaves* . . .: a ms. version has 'Wind-scattered laurel leaves', and a reference to Aeneid VI. I have restored the reference.

168 *Aeneid VI.4–901*: entitled 'Aeneid VI' in *Fossil Unicorn*. I have restored the full title from the ms.: it points to Vergil's recurring line which frames Book VI's narrative.

169 *Wyatt*: I have restored the space before the last line from a ms. version.

174 *Cranaë*: the epigraph from Homer and the space before the last line are restored from a ms.

Uncollected Poems

177 *Coasting by a citadel*: the ms. has in the margin '(Rutilius)'. It is not a translation but a side-glance at Rutilius's long poem *De reditu suo*, an account of his sea-journey from Rome to Gaul, written in the early fifth century AD.

193 *Initiation*: from *Six Oxford Poets*, Bodleian Library, 1977.

194 *First Mystery*: from *Argo* I.2, 1979.

214 *Ruffling the field's uneasy fur* . . .: the epigraph is from Yeats. See the note on 'Robert Kirk', p. 244.

217 *Tonn Tuili*: the phrase, meaning 'the flood-tide's wave', is from the early Irish 'Lament of the Old Woman of Beare'.

Translations

233 Sally Purcell made versions from Anyte and Nossis, two of the earliest women poets (roughly contemporary with Theokritos), for my *The Greek Anthology* (1973). She contributed thirteen poems to the book.

235 *Eirenaios, ἀγκὰς ἐλοῦσά μ' ἔχεις*: a later poem from the Palatine (Greek) Anthology, 5.249, omitting the first two lines about Rhodopë's abandonment of her pride in the face of Aphodite's arrows. Irenaeus was an official at Justinian's court. I do not know why she made this version in French.

237 *'Come uccel peregrin che il lito amato . . .'*: I have been unable to trace the source of this poem.

Index of Titles